CW00643810

Her essence in our senses—is music
that's measured in verses,
Ballads, new triads like trees
Reaching through time with riches.
Menna Elfyn

Trying The Line

A volume of tribute to
Gillian Clarke

Edited by
Menna Elfyn

GOMER

First Impression—June 1997

ISBN 1 85902 585 4

This volume has been produced with the support of the Arts Council of Wales

Printed at
Gomer Press, Llandysul, Ceredigion

CONTENTS

Introduction

One may well ask why it was felt necessary to celebrate the work of an eminent poet with this *cyfrol deyrnged*, a volume of tribute, to mark her sixtieth birthday. It is far better to celebrate, noted one black writer jokingly, than to *be* celebrated. Be that as it may, in the last few years an old tradition of praise and celebration has found new expression in Wales in the form of events and books which celebrate the achievements of our writers—such charismatic figures as the late Gwyn A. Williams and Glyn Jones, and the omnipresent Tony Conran. For those who contributed to these celebrations there was a great sense of pride in being able to unite in solidarity and marvel at the creative energy of the artists, representatives of a most ancient craftspeople. This volume of tribute, however, differs from those events in the simple fact that we are celebrating a woman writer. The time has come in the history of literature when women writers do not disappear into oblivion or die in obscurity!

And the younger the subject of the celebration, the more joyous the occasion. Sixty is an interesting age, after all: too old to parade in the pretence of being young and yet too young for people to believe that the most ambitious work has necessarily been accomplished. From Gillian Clarke, a late starter when it came to publishing her work, but one whose craft develops and finds new modes of expression with each passing year, there is no doubt a great deal of fine writing yet to come. Recalling all her creative activities over the past ten years left me breathless. The breadth of her output has included most of the writing genres: a volume of poetry, short stories for anthologies, a libretto, at least two plays, editorship of two children's anthologies, translation of poetry for a Welsh language poet, as well as the completion of an English version of Kate Roberts's novel, *Tegwch y Bore*. All of this, as well as the workaday job of running creative writing workshops in schools and colleges and the more prestigious readings at International Festivals.

The critical essays in this volume will provide the reader with further testimony of the range of Gillian's achievements, not only as a writer herself but as a motivator of others—in her roles as editor, tutor and one of the founders of Tŷ Newydd Writers' Centre. In addition to this, I would like to draw attention to three elements which in my view have made Gillian Clarke's presence in the literary life of Wales such an enriching one.

As a poet, Gillian has never denied the power of gender. Her exploration of womanist themes in works such as 'Letter from a far Country' offered a new understanding of subject matter that might in the past have been regarded as not central to life, or not profound enough to be the stuff of poetry. She has not only inspired other woman writers to realise the depth of such material, but also increased the awareness in readers of the richness of a woman poet's life.

I first came across Gillian Clarke's work by chance, on overhearing a remark by my mother's neighbour about a poet she'd heard reading her work in Carmarthen. What impressed her was the way the poet had shown little regard for her own talent at the beginning of her writing career and had even thrown her poems into the bin, from where they had to be retrieved by someone else, who then passed them on to be published. The story stuck in my mind for days. Such honesty was so rare that I remember feeling a sense of kindred spirit: I too at that time was wrestling with my own petty efforts. As a Welsh language writer in the mid-seventies, the term 'Poetry Reading' meant very little to me. In Welsh language circles at least, I sensed that there was very little communication between poets and their public. If you were considered a poet of any standing that is exactly what you did —stand on a stage, to the full awe of the audience, talking about the lesser mortals who had braved the competition in question.

Gillian Clarke's great strides with reading in public and communicating with an audience has surely enlarged the audience in Wales and further afield. Her commitment to turning listeners into writers, and passive audiences into readers is surely without rival. She also moved other writers to turn their abilities to similar activities—running workshops, tutoring—and many found sustenance from such sources for lifestyles that even at the best of times are lean and solitary. However, not everyone was able to share her enthusiasm all of the time. Often, driving home from a shared residency, I would be totally negative at some of the day's achievements and feeling a little cheated that I had given so much with so little reward. Gillian, on the other hand, would always be positive about the day, recalling images and ideas with incredible ecstasy. One sensed a love for poetry that was at times evangelical, and Gillian would surely add that everyone could be saved.

The third aspect of Gillian Clarke's achievements to which I would like to pay tribute is her work as ambassador for Wales in the wider world. Wherever she has met fellow writers or given readings of her poetry, her commitment to Welshness and to the Welsh language has been pivotal in moving people towards a clearer understanding of the vibrancy of a language under threat, and the whole identity of Welshness along with it. There have been times when I have felt ashamed of the lack of assertiveness in the Welsh and wish to God to have been born to some other tribe! Gillian, always positive and assertive, has always managed to dispel such scepticism, berating those who did not respect the bicultural situation in Wales. At international gatherings and readings she always carried Wales in her heart and often on her tongue. A few years ago she delivered a poem in Welsh and English at Poetry International Rotterdam, the most prestigious of all world poetry events. Her international standing is surely to the benefit of contemporary Welsh literature in both languages and her abilities as judge is very much sought after. Her belief in cultures and languages being allowed to thrive is neatly expressed in an editorial note in *The Anglo-Welsh Review* which affirms her uncompromising stance:

> It is not enough to praise landscape, for Wales is made not of stones but of people and language.

Gillian Clarke's sense of loss at being denied the language at an early age has been distilled into a deep understanding of Welsh identity in all its variety, and into a desire for its survival and growth. The vibrancy of her poetry and other writing in prose has been a sustaining element in our culture, one that has helped to encapsulate a Wales that celebrates ethnicity and diversity. At an inaugural meeting to promote the idea of a New Welsh Language Act in Cardiff in 1985 Gillian delivered a passionate speech about the need for Welshness, which reminded one very much of Simone Weil's insistence on The Need for Roots.

I have tried to adhere to her contribution to Welsh literature and Wales lest my tribute to her be seen as less than (as that ambivalent term would have it) objective. I could have dwelt on her kindnesses, to a whole range of people amongst whom poets would be in the majority, I'm sure. Her dedication also to the well-being of other writers seems to be part of her unwritten job description as poet/seer. Of late, as if she had time, she took on another task to add to her workload, namely that of translating other people's work, a task which offers so little in return. Yet she undertakes these tasks so ungrudgingly, her motive perhaps being best expressed in another editorial comment:

> A commitment to literature often sends a writer out on the road. Some things writers do for an income . . . some for modest payment and a duty to literature; others we do for love only, editing, sitting on committees, answering endless mail.

Again this expresses the struggle with responsibilities, be they small or large, and the total dedication to the art of being a writer. She once remarked that 'we' was far more common in Welsh literature than the 'I' of English literature because there was more of a sense of community. It could also be that she, woman, mother, grandmother, sister is more used to the collective term than the solipsistic tendency of other writers. Whatever the correct reason for the usage, 'we' in Gillian's work and life has been about sharing and making connections, in order to reach the ever-faithful—or not so faithful—in the fold.

I was once chided by one of my translators (not easy to guess who!) for saying that literature is all about generosity. Not, he replied curtly, when it interferes with your critical judgement. Being aware of that danger has possibly made me more critical of poet friends than of strangers, but I am ready to assert that in Gillian's case it is with critical judgement at work when reading her poems that a great sense of giving is to be felt.

It may be the downside of being a small nation that we are sometimes unwilling to praise, even though the purpose of most of the early Welsh poetry was to give praise. England has its honours to bestow on the worthy, but Gillian is hardly likely to crave a visit to the Palace. The Eisteddfod, too, has its honours list but the contribution to Welsh writing in English is not yet recognised by the Gorsedd of the Bards.

In the meantime, this slim volume will enable those who admire Gillian Clarke's work to enjoy a tribute by writers and critics in recognition of her achievements over many years. Moreover, for those who wish to make a study of her work, the bibliography will prove invaluable. I am indebted to all the contributors for the poems, personal essays and criticism which together reflect the considerable influence Gillian Clarke has had on a diverse community of writers and readers.

Although it has been for very small financial reward, Gillian Clarke has, nevertheless, managed to make a living solely from her writing, albeit a modest one. Writing is all about a different kind of wealth, say writers at times, and yet then we despair when it is difficult to make ends meet. Yet Gillian Clarke is a giver of jewels—or ram skulls if you are so inclined!—as well as a giver of words that sound out even to 'deaf men singing' (Dannie Abse).

And since she is only sixty I'm inclined to add, after her new departure into prose writing and playmaking, there are great things yet to come. Gillian: *bendith arnat.*

Menna Elfyn

Deaf Men Singing
(to Gillian)

Most poems, like golems, turn to dust at dawn
but you hallow the coarse endeavour, attend
the awkward, the not winging, the also-rans;
cheer Z because it's last; salute deaf men singing
who feels a piano's wood to hear its song,
myopic painters, their details clearly wrong,
their vast perspectives to a No-Man's Past.

Inhuman angels may command perfection
but the hollow circle drawn by Giotto
would have been more genial if hand had wavered.
So you commend sweet error, would not mend
the nervous junction, convert the letter O
to Death's infrangible and favoured number,
with its unseen beginning, no evident end.

Dannie Abse

13

Milky Way, Llanystumdwy*
(for Gillian Clarke)

'You think Wales is weird? Come outside n take
a look at this . . .' The city kids from England,
   wise their teen lives
to noise-lit streets, the night-free nights, grope
down towards the garden. 'Look at what, Gordon Bennett?'
   'This.' 'What?' 'This, the sky . . .'

No moon, no street glare: crystal the dark, a silence on us
   as eyes that heard tell but never saw
         widen to the Way,
         drink deep the milk
of our galactic home, splashed rim to chalice rim through
         disposable night

. . . two hundred thousand million suns . . .
dust, gas . . . the matter factories . . .

'I had forgotten . . .'
               'I never knew . . .'

. . . and Andromeda, the neighbour light
fresh to the eye as
               cold to the toes
               through wet sneakers,
on track to us
from times pre-human,
               two million light years abroad . . .

Caer Gwydion, Caer Arianrhod . . .
'What is it all?
            Where are we?'
A garden,

14

a garden in the Square of Pegasus,
with lamps at sea
        and cows chomping cud,
     every few minutes the splattering of shit, a
—shooting star—

Tonight, boys and girls, we could build Stonehenge.

Nigel Jenkins

* This poem sprang from the first writing course I tutored with Gillian—for
children from Holt and Forest Schools in Wokingham, Berkshire, at Tŷ
Newydd in September 1990.

Oratorio as Prelude

(A review of *The King of Britain's Daughter*)

Gillian Clarke first came into prominence in the Seventies as a poet who dealt vividly with experience. She cut her textures with a sharp knife: her poems were lively and crisp on the tongue. Even in those days, though, there was a sense that what she was really interested in was the whole nexus of feelings which underlay these single experiences—building herself into myth, as it were, as woman, as poet, and as only partly disinherited heir of Welsh countryside life. 'Birth' for instance, about the birth of a calf:

> I could feel the soft sucking
> Of the new-born, the tugging pleasure
> Of bruised reordering, the signal
> Of milk's incoming tide, and satisfaction
> Fall like a clean sheet around us.

(A lot of her poetry could be described as 'bruised reordering' as much as 'tugging pleasure'.) In the present volume, we have another lyric about the birth of a calf—this time much more casual about the rawness of her feelings. Significantly (in a book where father and brother figures are well to the fore) it is entitled 'Vet':

> I got off lightly that time,
> no knife, no severing,
> no inter-uterine butchery
> to cut them free.
>
> He let go the rope of water
> and the calf swam home like a salmon
> furled in a waterfall,
> gleaming, silver, sweet under the tongue
> of his brimming mother.

16

The later vision includes the earlier and yet preserves also the sense of the everyday surface. Perhaps the male figures in this new book*, 'the Kings of Britain' whose daughter she is, are to be felt as catalysts, connections between the everyday and the mythological—both of which *are* women's worlds, of course, as 'Letter from a Far Country' demonstrates: the ordering ('You'll find my inventories pinned/inside all of the cupboard doors') but also that note 'that only we can hear' that children sing.

Her father slips in and out of the Otherworld like a Celtic god, bringing connection between myth and her childhood, while the mothers washed and hung clothes to dry, and sometimes gave away talismans too old and shabby for their ordering to countenance, like her father's hat:

> When she gave it away
>
> —it was old, the tweed threadbare,
> the gold words faded like old books
> inside the headband—
>
> she gave away mornings of forage,
> beachcombings, blackberries, pebbles, eggs,
> field-mushrooms with pleated linings,
>
> his fist working it to a form
> for the leveret that quivered under my hand
> before it died.

It has been fascinating to watch how the individual isolating lyric has been superseded as a centre of interest in Gillian Clarke's work by more holistic or symphonic structures in which many and disparate experiences cohere. (This may have feminist as well as Celtic and literary implications, I don't know: certainly 'Blood' in this volume, which seems to me one of her finest poems, is a 'symphonic'

* *The King of Britain's Daughter*, Carcanet, 1994

sequence dealing centrally with women's experience.) She has used the 'letter in a bottle' formula to articulate the 'hidden' history of women; and the various forms of genealogy and *cofiant* to embody herself as an heir to centuries of Welsh life. For 'The King of Britain's Daughter' she was apparently inspired by a commission to write the text of an oratorio for the Hay-on-Wye Festival.

From a literary point of view, oratorio is halfway between lyric drama (unstaged opera) and choric narrative. Mostly texts seem to be *ad hoc* affairs, put together to hang music on. This oratorio was to tell the story from the Second Branch of the *Mabinogion*, of how the giant Bendigeidfran invaded Ireland to rescue his sister Branwen from the cruelty of the Irish court. Only two sections of the sequence—12, 'Branwen's Songs and the Lament of Bendigeidfran', and 13, 'Branwen's Grave'—are at all the sort of thing we'd expect from such a scheme; the rest are personal lyrics mostly about the poet's childhood and her relationship with her wireless-operator father Penri Williams.

The wonder is, how such disparate material could cohere at all—yet cohere it does, with a mutual relevance that is both moving and impressive. A poem about the radio on her parents' kitchen window-sill for example, ends:

> The news came out of the sky,
> a mist off the sea,
> an incoming shadow
> of rain or wings.

Gillian Clarke was a child in a wartime dominated by the wireless; this bringing together of Branwen's starling—the 'incoming shadow of wings'—and her father's radio has an extraordinary poignancy of 'ancestral voices prophesying war.' It is typical of the way her imagination fuses together the 'oratorio' myth and the personal lyric in a synthesis where metaphor becomes reality.

This 'oratorio', then, is her Prelude, her poem on the growth of the poetic imagination, inhabited by giants and wrecked boats, Concorde and wireless aerial, singing seals and Branwen's starling—and above all by her father, whose personality dominates the book as a kind of male muse bringing her poems. His own life is delicately, tentatively suggested. In a poem where she has swum out to sea and imagined meeting the Little Mermaid on her way to meet the prince, now

> Nothing
> breaks the surface of darkness or sea
> where we beached the boat so long ago,
> and I suddenly knew she slipped him,
> that he carried like an X-ray
> her shadow picture.
>
> A staircase in the sea
> and something gleaming in the deepest water.

It may be something to do with my own tastes, but of her three sequences, I find this the most satisfying, perhaps because it deals with imagination and childhood—which are certainly easier subjects for a poet—rather than female ordering or the mysterious relation we have with our forefathers.

Tony Conran
(first published in *New Welsh Review* 23, 1993)

Through the Telescope

October, and the nights were drawing in. Darkness gathering, and visibility poor. A damp summer had given way to a wet autumn, and here in the Teifi Valley the clouds were piling up thick and fast, driven in from the sea on depression after depression. A shadow in the west: Cruise Missiles being loaded onto the planes that would fly them into Greenham. They arrived on November 14th, the Feast of Kali. I noted it in my calendar. Coincidence, or Kali's own black humour? Or were there Hindus in the Pentagon?

Those of us, poor, principled and marginalised, who lived through the early eighties now look back to that time as if through some dark tunnel. It was easy to feel despair then, a year after Thatcher's landslide re-election, with the miners embarking on their long hopeless battle and everywhere greed, lies and self-interest. But we didn't despair, most of us. We got on with living: we sang and climbed fences at Greenham, we played with our children, we tended our gardens, fell in and out of love, just as always. And during that year, 1984, I started writing again.

It began in the spring, this urge to write poems: an act of assertion, a way of fighting back with some kind of counter-spell. It was surprisingly easy to start again, after a break of some ten years in which I'd married wrongly straight from university, had a wild sort of breakdown, emerged tougher, tried living in communes, ran away with my present partner, had two babies in quick succession and came to my father's country and an unknown future. We spent what money we had on a tiny two-hundred year-old cottage on the lower flanks of Llanllwni mountain. It sounds romantic from this distance, but we were there from necessity. It was pretty grim in the winter, or when it rained, which was most of the time. It was dark in there, surrounded by walls two feet thick and deep small windows, and with ceilings so low even I could reach up and touch the beams without stretching. Doorways built in the days when grown men were no more than my height, five foot four, just. Nelson was only five foot, and he wasn't even Welsh.

It was like living in a cave, and we felt like troglodytes, or some species of snail, hidden under a stone. The first winter we were there, 1982/3, we had to heat all our water in a black iron kettle: there was one cold tap over the stone sink in the rotting kitchen extension. Next summer we acquired a rusty Rayburn for £30 and a copper hotwater cylinder, and plumbed in some warmth. We connected ourselves—unofficially —to the mains drainage (an unpleasant tale, best avoided at dinner parties). We replaced the crumbling window frames with handmade sashes, one at a time. We cleared the garden —across the main road from the house—of junk and old tractor parts and began to grow vegetables. We even kept a few chickens for a while, but they kept getting out and eating the vegetables. We went on expeditions to Brechfa Forest with Reinallt, a friend with a van, to scrounge firewood. We had baths in the zinc tub in front of the fire—nice and cosy, but a little awkward for visitors. We sent the children to the Ysgol Feithrin in Gwyddgrug: first Rowan, then Biddy; then at four to the village school, Welsh-speaking as a matter of course. The other mothers were polite but wary; curious, but keeping their distance. Where did we come from? Nowhere in particular—too many places before here. What did my husband do? Gardening, house repairs, childcare, washing, woodcutting, breadmaking, carpentry . . . nothing, no job at present.

'Whatever will you do with yourself when your youngest starts school?' they'd ask. I wanted to say, 'I'll write'—but that sounded too weird. The other mothers had part-time jobs helping with school dinners or cleaning at the hospital. The great ambition was to get a job at the new Marks and Spencer in Carmarthen. They talked to each other and their friends on CB radios when I went round for coffee—in English, part of the code. I felt I was treading water, waiting for something to happen.

Sometime in the summer of '84, after I'd written a couple of poems and was wondering what to do about it, I saw an article in *The Guardian* featuring a woman poet from Wales called Gillian Clarke. There was a photograph—hand propping chin, a flirtatious smile, long dark hair streaked with grey. She'd had children. She'd had difficulties to contend with: a divorce, insecurity. She didn't publish any poems till she was in her thirties . . . I was in my thirties! I *had* had poems published, years before, but I'd been afraid I'd left it too late to make a new start. Now here was this successful poet saying it wasn't too late, that women are often late-comers to poetry through force of circumstance, and that women's writing and women's concerns were important. Women should write from their own lives, she said, and this was every bit as valuable as anything men had to say. I gave a small cheer, and poured myself a glass of homemade wine. On our next trip to the library, I borrowed a copy of Gillian's *Letter From a Far Country*. It was the first book of contemporary poetry I'd read for almost ten years, and the first by a living woman. I was aware of women's writing in a general way, of course. My friend Janet Dubé had drawn my attention to some of Menna Elfyn's poems in translation, powerful and full of spirit. Perhaps something was going on round here after all.

But Gillian Clarke lived in Cardiff, according to the article, and without a car or money to spare I never expected to meet her. Cardiff was a far country as far as I was concerned.

I wrote another poem, about standing with my hands in the sink with the autumn leaves turning gold outside, watching poems spill from my fingers into the soapy water, to drain away down the plughole. I was frustrated and obscurely angry. I felt stuck and invisible. The wall of the farmer's field came right up to the back of our house, leaving us just enough room to squeeze past the back door and window. The busy Carmarthen to Lampeter road ran past the little cobbled yard at the front. We shared the yard with the couple next door. We shared half the garden across the road with them too. We were hemmed in on all sides, the middle section of what had been a small farmhouse. There was the mountain sloping up to the east, and hills to the north and south—only the west was open to the treeline and astonishing sunsets. I wanted room to expand, but there didn't seem to be anywhere to expand into.

Around this time my partner was trying to get an unemployed self-help group together. We knew there were people in the area in similar circumstances to ours, locals as well as incomers, and it seemed a good idea to get together to share views and resources and skills. These days we'd have started a LETS group, but they hadn't been invented. A few people turned up, including a soft-spoken diffident man who identified himself as a poet: Douglas Houston. Douglas lived a mile down the lane from us, in a rented house with his wife and two small boys. He was trying to finish a PhD on Auden and Heaney. I'd heard of Seamus Heaney but I'd never read his poems. Douglas didn't blink at my ignorance. We arranged to swap some poems. His seemed terrifyingly well-wrought and were packed with intellect and a dry, painful wit. The ones I understood were strangely moving. He was kind about mine and treated them seriously. He spoke articulately about them: what he liked, and why. I'd never had that kind of feedback before.

Next week Douglas called round in some excitement to say he'd heard that a writers' group was starting in Lampeter, run by Gillian Clarke. She had a residency at the University, and was starting the group as part of it, to all comers. It seemed too good to be true. Suddenly something was moving—did I dare take advantage of this? We had no car just then, but Douglas offered to drive me. I summoned up my courage: it would have been churlish to refuse.

And so it began. Others who passed through that group—
some who still go there more than twelve years on—have their
own story, but this is how it began for me: terrified, clutching
a handful of poems, fighting nausea as Douglas swung the car
round the bends, rain and darkness lashing the windscreen.
He used to drive taxis in Germany, he told me; so that's why
we were on the wrong side of the road half the time. When
we arrived and found the small room my mouth was dry and
I knew I'd be unable to read anything if asked. Gillian was
there, smiling, older than I expected—the dark hair had
mysteriously become white. Well, I thought, if I had a
publisher using a sexy-looking photo of me that was past its
sell-by date, I certainly wouldn't object. That little bit of
vanity pleased me: she was only human after all. Always, from
the start, there were these chinks of vulnerability in Gillian. I
don't think she always intended them to show, but it made it
easy for me to warm to her.

I don't remember much about that first session. Sue
Moules was there, looking nervous but already seeming at
home, and Kathy Miles. Kathy read a spare, interesting
poem, with her head down and her hands shaking. So I
wasn't the only one to be scared to death that evening.
Gillian spoke reassuringly. She spoke about how she
envisaged the group, as a company of equals, writing to a
suggested theme in our own time at home, sharing the results
each week, plus anything else we wanted to workshop in the
group. She said she was just facilitating the process, not
'teaching' us or imposing her views on us. In fact, and
inevitably, Gillian led the group with the force of her
personality from day one: but the principle of mindful
attention to each other's work, with constructive criticism and
appreciation, held good all the time I was there—five years in
all—and by all accounts survives to this day.

At the end of that first evening. Gillian asked if anyone had
any work to leave with her till next week. Shyly I handed her
my half-dozen poems. Next week, not only had she read

everyone's work, but she handed it back with verbal and written comments. She was positive and encouraging to everyone, but I hadn't expected the praise she gave to mine. 'I wish I'd written some of these myself!' she said, picking out the poems in the sink one for special mention. This was probably more than they deserved, but it gave me the boost I needed. I realised by the end of the evening that I had a reason to write, and the impetus to keep me at it. I wasn't invisible and wordless any more.

Those first few months at Gillian's group were what turned me into a writer, rather than merely someone who sometimes wrote poems. For one thing, I was sprung out of myself and my private world and forced to consider an audience. Years of living on the margins, cooped up in poverty with very small children, had turned me somewhat agoraphobic. The wider world attracted me and scared me at the same time. I was reluctant to go out and mix with people; but when I did I received such a charge of energy, such a buzz. It was like gorging on something I'd been starved of. In those early days, when I got home from the writing group I'd often develop a splitting headache, or I'd collapse with exhaustion the next day. The energy charge was so strong I couldn't handle it. It was worse than being in love: no, my memory plays tricks—it was exactly the same. And I discovered I had something to give, to share, and I was getting something back: response, interest, attention, praise, knowledge, inspiration. Isn't that what every writer wants? Why else do we do it?

Gillian gave all that and more, and so did the other members of the group. I particularly remember 'Smoky' (Ann Price-Owen), Geoff Constable, Michael Chorost from America, Anne Grimes, Andrew Hassan, and a guy from the other side of Newcastle Emlyn, a wood-turner . . . and Doug Houston of course, perhaps the sharpest and most perceptive critic of anyone there at that time. Exchanging ideas and writings, that needling edge of competition, plus the constant need to listen intelligently, also helped make a writer of me.

And reading, reading, reading all the stuff I'd been missing out on.

Then there was the weekly topic or theme, in poetry or prose, a subject to write around, a hook to hang something on; and Gillian's emphasis on not waiting around for inspiration, but to just do it and see what happens. There was always that deadline of next Tuesday, and the need to make it good enough to read out—that is, satisfying my own criteria and up to my own required standard, which was rising steadily. I junked so much stuff that wasn't up to scratch, rather than read it out. I needed the discipline: I also needed the excuse of 'having' to write something for next week's workshop, in order to shut myself in the bedroom away from chores and distractions for a few hours each week. Time for myself, that somehow I couldn't ask for in any other way. So poems were written that would never have got written otherwise.

Undoubtedly the most powerful factor of all for me was Gillian herself. Her open regard for my work led me to believe in myself, and her successful example provided me with the perfect model I needed. I found her extraordinarily generous. Her coaxing encouraged me to send poems out to magazines. My first success was with the Anglo-Welsh Review, edited by Greg Hill. He took a poem I'd written in the spring of '84, before the group existed: 'The Song of Blodeuwedd on May Morning'. I still read it sometimes. Gillian insisted that I take my craft seriously, and that I think of myself as a poet by profession—something that seemed almost too audacious then. It was Gillian who encouraged me to publish a sequence of poems I wrote through 1985 and shared each month with the group, one every twenty-eight days: *The Tree Calendar*. It became the basis for my first collection, helped to birth by Gillian's midwifery skill.

Much as I admired—and admire—Gillian, I didn't always agree with her. She liked to make generalisations that I was sure couldn't be universally applied. I got to recognise her favourite themes, her pet hates, her cherished notions; but I was getting the confidence to form my own opinions, and wasn't too put out if hers were different. I valued her approval of what I wrote, but I was writing for myself, not for Gillian. There were some people who wrote, I thought, far too much to please her. Other people who didn't quite fit were subtly excluded in a way that troubled me. The group became very safe, very comfortable, always enjoyable, but perhaps too predictable. After a few years it became a bit like a family, with Gillian as the mother, rebellious kids and all. I wasn't sure I wanted to be part of that. Perhaps, I think now, what I really want is to lead, not to follow. There would have been tensions with that, if I'd stayed too long. My very success—publications, prizes, readings,—although feted by the group and largely arising from my involvement with the group, became embarrassing to me, a barrier I was afraid might stand between myself and less experienced or less confident writers. When we moved house to live in the Gwendraeth Valley it was too far to go to Lampeter for an evening. I think this probably happened at about the right time.

But the Lampeter group was a tremendous catalyst for me. Gillian was the guide and model I needed; in her sensitivity she intuited that, and she gave without stinting. I shall never forget that.

The group still meets on Tuesday nights in term time. Scores of good writers have passed through, for long or short seasons. There have been three simply-produced anthologies over the years, but now Chris Ozzard, mover and shaker, is completing the production of a major anthology spanning the best writing from the group's history, and he's looking for a commercial publisher.

I've been tutoring creative writing, and especially poetry, for ten years now, in schools and with adults—though nowhere near on Gillian's scale: I haven't the stamina and drive, and there's too much else in my life still claiming my attention.

I've developed my own style and approach, and I've learnt from all the writers I've worked with over the years; but I've reached this point due to the confidence I developed in Gillian's group, a light in the shadows as it was for me then.

To think of that time now: those rides through the dark of that first winter, talking poetry (often literally, with Doug Houston reciting chunks of his own and other people's verse from memory, word-perfect), the heater blasting away, the black hedges streaking by, the moon bobbing alongside.

To think of writing in the cramped bedroom, at the old oak desk I picked up from a warehouse in Liverpool in another life, a fur coat wrapped around my knees against the cold. Grey light seeping in at floor level from the window, a low doorway onto the world. Slaughterhouse lorries with their hidden victims, forestry lorries full of logs, cars hurrying past. Writing another poem for the Tree Calendar, my self-imposed task to take me through a hard year.

To think of the house we lived in, a sort of womb in which all this was gestating. Rain. Chernobyl. Fortnightly giros. The children growing up fast. Battling with mud, traffic, illness; but then the unsurpassed beauties; days of sun, long soft dusks, the stars' unending pathways. Gillian and Dave coming round for supper one summer evening: I made a lavish trifle which Gillian tucked into with gusto. Drink loosening our tongues. Gillian laughing, girlish. Us visiting their house for supper in their garden and Gillian showing my children the moon through her telescope. They still remember that. Drinking too much of their delicious sloe gin. Feeling unaccountably sad the next day: so much that can't be reached, those glimpses of something deeper behind the easy conviviality. Why do poets lead such isolated lives? What do we fear from each other? Is that something a group like Lampeter's tries to redress, to heal, or to disguise?

To think of all that time is to recall an adventure; something I've travelled through, that enriched me, that I've survived able to tell the tale. Encountering Gillian then was a fateful occurrence. For me she was the wise woman at the crossroads bearing a gift, perhaps a box of curious workmanship, to be opened when most in need. I've opened that box a few times. Thank you, Gillian. I'm not at all sure where I'm heading, but I wouldn't be on this road if it wasn't for your companionship along the way.

The group continues under Gillian's tutelage; writing is still alive in Lampeter. There is still the annual party in July. Each year I think I may go, but forget to ask exactly where and when it's taking place this time . . . perhaps I'm reluctant to go back and find it doesn't fit my expectations; or that, having shut the door behind me, like Alice I'll find I've grown too big for the house and can't get back in. Looking into the past can be like looking down the wrong end of a telescope to view a world in miniature, shining small and very far away. Or a series of eggs to be broken out of, each bigger than the last. Driving through New Inn, as I do from time to time—or on the Traws Cambria bus on my way to or from Tŷ Newydd—I pass our cottage and it looks ridiculously tiny, not a real house at all, a gnomish dwelling or a child's *tŷ bach twt*.

It's seven years since we left. Now it's spring 1997, and the long shadows seem to be lifting. Gillian, youthful Gemini, will be sixty in June. In only a couple of years I'll be the same age she was in that autumn of 1984, and I still feel my best years are ahead of me; but the future rests on what has gone before.

Maybe that image of the shrinking past and the eggshells is all wrong: maybe the further back you look, the bigger it gets. It all depends on which end of the telescope you're looking through.

Hilary Llewellyn-Williams

A Bunch of Flowers

for Gillian

Sunflowers, *blodau'r haul*, Vincent's
blazing asterisks

Pabi Cymru, poppy of Wales,
our own bright solar discs

Pagoda'd foxgloves, *bysedd y cŵn*,
with purple finger-stalls

Roman red valerian,
triaglog, topping walls

Dewi's golden daffodils,
soundless trumpets of spring

Yellowflag, *iris felen*,
poised on canary wing

Bluebells heard by cuckoos,
clychau'r gog, in a green glade

Galaxies of anemones
starring the birchgrove's shade

Flowers of Blodeuwedd: broom,
oak, foaming meadowsweet

Olwen's clover, *meillion*,
springing at her feet

Clotted cream of primroses,
briallu, under the hedge

Geranium, cardinal scarlet,
hot on the window-ledge.

Raymond Garlick

The Anglo-Welsh Review—Gillian Clarke as Editor

I first met Gillian Clarke when I was a student at Aberystwyth and the organiser of the newly resuscitated Alun Lewis Society. Ned Thomas had just launched a degree component course in the Literature of Twentieth Century Wales and we were enthusiastically inviting writers to address members of the society. Jeremy Hooker, who was also teaching at Aberystwyth during this period, advised us of suitable poets who would be prepared to read their work and enter into discussions with students about the process of writing. He particularly recommended Gillian Clarke. She was duly invited, came and did not disappoint our expectations. She not only gave us an insight into what she was about as a writer in Wales, but encouraged the would-be writers amongst us to join the fray. She came to us primarily as a poet who would read her own poetry but it was very much on the minds of those of us who wrote poetry ourselves that she was also an editor of a magazine that published poetry. I know I was not the only one to send work for consideration to *The Anglo-Welsh Review* as a result of that and her subsequent visits to Aberystwyth. Nor was I the only one to benefit from her sympathetic response and constructive comments on the work submitted. Gillian is herself on record as saying that discovering magazines like *The Anglo-Welsh Review* as a young aspiring poet 'gave me a sense of my own ability to join the ranks of the writers within them'.[1] Having become editor of the magazine she never forgot that important role of encouraging and giving space to emerging talent.

It was some time later as a post-graduate student that I suddenly became more acutely aware of how I might make my presence felt in the pages of *The Anglo-Welsh Review*. A new Reviews Editor was needed and my name had emerged as a possible candidate. Gillian asked to meet for an informal chat during which she managed to convince me that this was a job I both could and should take on. It was not long before I inherited several bulging files full of outstanding reviews and details of more in the pipeline together with a boxful of new books. My initial informal interview with Gillian some weeks before this had been a positive 'new horizons' affair. I had, of course, been briefed in the precise details of what was required and I must have given assurances that I could cope. Now those precise details had become actual problems. Previous reviews editors had built up a definitive collection of reviews of practically every book either published in Wales or of Welsh interererest. Roland Mathias reports in his essay 'The Lonely Editor' that Gillian jokingly 'alleged that she took over just in time to prevent me from having reviewed a book on snails because it had been written by a Welshman'.[2] I'm not sure of the public provenance of that comment but I had come across an earlier report of it in a review of Gillian's *The Sundial* in my local newspaper at about this time. There had clearly been an attempt to establish the magazine as a definitive record of Welsh cultural life in the widest possible sense under the editorship of Roland Mathias. But the number of pages available for reviews had been reduced and could no longer support this. I spoke to Gillian and proposed a drastic solution. I would use what I could in the next issue and send everything else in the files back to the reviewers in order to start from scratch.

Gillian's 'snail' joke suggested she would support me in this. Not only did she do so but she also encouraged me to take just those sorts of decision in order to give the reviews section my own emphasis and shape. In retrospect it became clear that Gillian wanted a Reviews Editor who would eventually move across to editing the main part of the magazine. So, with due respect to the tradition of the Review as a long-established journal, and also within the considerable restraints imposed by the printer/publishers, I worked myself into the job helped but not interfered with. She herself had served a similar apprenticeship under Roland Mathias, recording in her first editorial after he had left her in charge that 'He trained his apprentice with patience and kindness, imparting a respect for meticulous accuracy . . . never before experienced by one inclined to be more creative than careful'.[3] That was in 1976, although she had jointly edited the magazine with Roland Mathias since the fiftieth issue in 1973, having become Reviews Editor in 1971. In fact numbers from 1974 onwards invite contributors to send poetry and short stories to Gillian rather than Roland who appears to have dealt mainly with critical articles and features from this time.

Those, then, were the standards she set about applying to the training of her own apprentice, although I was not the first. She had, I think instinctively, chosen a fellow poet for her first Reviews Editor. Certainly Roland Mathias subsequently felt that she had given greater prominence to poetry on taking over as editor.[4] John Davies remained in the job for three years, not quite long enough to move from editing reviews to choosing other poets to appear in the magazine. His successor, Tony Bianchi, lasted for one year before pursuing his career in the Welsh Arts Council. Perhaps by then Gillian was ready to relinquish sole control of the editorial reins. It was not, anyway, very many years before she began to ask my opinion about items she was considering and eventually to use me as a filter when the weight of submissions was particularly heavy. By 1985 we were editing alternate issues. The distance between Aberystwyth and Cardiff might have made this difficult as submitted material had to pass back and forth between us, but luckily Gillian had other reasons to visit Aberystwyth regularly so this potential difficulty never arose.

As far as practical matters were concerned the apprenticeship was relatively painless. Gillian was a sympathetic teacher and I was an eager learner. What I'm not sure that I ever really learned to do with Gillian's consummate skill was to master the art of the helpful rejection slip. Of course there are some writers who do not wish to receive advice on their submissions, preferring simply to be told whether they are accepted or not. Any editor whose practice is to explain why work is not accepted will have experienced the curt response from those who feel they being patronised. I'm sure Gillian did not manage to entirely escape that experience. But I am equally sure that no small number of emerging poets benefited from the necessarily brief, but always encouraging, comments she made when sending work back. What she never did, and I hope I never did either, was to give anyone the impression that a rejection was absolute. It does not take much to add 'do try again' to an apology for not accepting work, but given the sheer bulk of material received by poetry editors (much, it seems, from people who do not themselves read poetry magazines) there is little incentive for them to do anything to encourage more submissions from any but the highest quality sources. Except, of course, a dedication to the craft of the poet and a determination to do all that is possible to nurture the impulse to develop that craft wherever it arises.

Quite clearly the qualities that have made Gillian so much in demand as a creative writing tutor, both in Wales and farther afield, also made her a good editor. She was a friend to poets and made her magazine a haven for their work. In spite of her growing fame as a poet in her own right beyond Wales, and the fact that we often received submissions from those who had attended her Arvon Foundation courses in England, she was always also conscious of the importance of *The Anglo-Welsh Review* as an expression of the literary culture of Wales. This did not mean not accepting work from English poets, but the ethos of the magazine was always to be Welsh. That anonymous review of *The Sundial* in my local paper also stated that she had 'made literature rather than the author's Welsh origins the main reason for inclusion'. This was undoubtedly true, but her editorials often addressed issues in Welsh life and one consisted of an editorial petition in favour of devolution. Judging by my subsequent experience I can imagine that one might have required some delicate handling of the publishers who were always a little touchy about even the most mildly controversial of editorial opinions. It has to be said that neither of us was particularly well-served by the publisher's inability to keep to the agreed publication schedule, or the general insentivity to the niceties of layout. Sometimes I felt that Gillian simply sailed above such matters, accepting them as an inevitable part of life and therefore never allowing herself to be upset by them. But I'm sure this was simply the positive outlook which she always maintained despite such frustrations.

Gillian Clarke's status as a poet is beyond doubt. She has also earned a well-deserved reputation as a sensitive and helpful creative writing tutor. In retrospect her shorter career as an editor may not seem so important. But it has to be seen in the context of the attempt to create a literary life, a life lived by and for literature. Few are able to live such a life with any sort of integrity, particularly in Wales where the opportunities to earn a living by doing so are even more restricted. But that is what Gillian has attempted and the editorship of a literary magazine is one part of the mosaic of activities which make up that life. And a *literary* magazine is what *The Anglo-Welsh Review* was under her editorship. The main focus was the poems and these always came first. Next the short stories. Then the critical articles. Finally the reviews. That was an ordering which reflected editorial priorites. I remember someone saying to me once that Gillian was convinced of the importance of literature, that it was an essential part of life rather than simply an amusement or a diversion which enriched life. He said he envied her this belief as she could not himself hold it. I think there is some truth in this observation. Many people, even those active in literary circles, would not feel able to give literature in general and poetry in particular this primacy. I like to think I do, but cannot say that my own life as a teacher of the subject quite reflects the single-minded devotion that Gillian has shown. It is one thing to idealise a literary life, quite another to live it.

NOTES

[1] Interview with Gillian Clarke in *Common Ground* edited by Susan Butler (Poetry Wales Press, 1985) p. 196.

[2] Roland Mathias *A Ride Through The Wood* (Poetry Wales Press, 1985) p. 303.

[3] Editorial to *The Anglo-Welsh Review* No. 57 (Autumn, 1976).

[4] Roland Mathias contributed an appreciation of Gillian's editorship of *The Anglo-Welsh Review* to the Editorial of No. 78 (Spring, 1985).

Greg Hill

Gulls
for Gillian

Gulls are glanced from the lift
Of cliffing air
And left
Loitering in the descending drift,
Or tilt gradient and go
Down steep invisible clefts in the grain
Of air, blading against the blow,

Back-flip, wisp
Over the foam-galled green
Building seas, and they scissor
Tossed spray, shave sheen,
Wing-waltzing their shadows
Over the green hollows.

Or rise again in the wind's landward rush
And, hurdling the thundering bush
With the stone wall flung in their faces,
Repeat their graces.

Ted Hughes

Penworker

My hand is cramped from penwork.
There is give in my sharp quill-point.
Its bird-mouth issues a dark
Blue, jet-bright runnel of ink.

God's shining wisdom streams
From my fine-drawn, sallow hand:
Riverrun on the vellum
Of ink from green-skinned holly.

My small runny pen keeps going
Across illuminated ground
To produce a treasured thing—
Penwork that cramps my hand.

Seamus Heaney
from the 11th century Irish

Training the Greenhorn

A tireless concern for the writing of others, and an immensely energetic striving to enable that writing to reach the quality to which it aspires, characterise the tutoring of Gillian Clarke. Her industry on the variety of courses she has tutored, and also with her own creative writing group in Lampeter, is testatment to this. Indeed, this latter is remarkable in the number of its members who have developed as writers, publishing in Wales and elsewhere.

On a personal level I am indebted to Gillian Clarke for the ways in which she fostered me as a greenhorn, not to say clueless, co-tutor at Lumb Bank and Tŷ Newydd. Today, almost everything I know about the typical 'creative writing week' at such places—especially the crucial details of its structuring—has been based on Gillian's own practices.

However, I would have to confess that I am somewhat less industrious than she. Certainly, I have clear memories of my first visit to Lumb Bank, the Arvon writing centre in rural West Yorkshire. There I partnered Gillian in charge of a group from Sheffield Girls High, with the necessary assistance of English teacher and writer, Rosie Ford. The ferocious log fire in the house's cavernous hearth; the Colden water, choked with boulders and the trunks of fallen alders, in spate beneath Range Wood; the trek uphill to the settlement of New Delight; the trek downhill through the garlicky air of the ransom-filled woodland to Hebden Bridge railway station; the grave of Sylvia Plath in Heptonstall churchyard (usually damaged by those protesting about the use of the surname 'Hughes' on the headstone): all remain vivid.

Yet what lingers most tellingly is the sense of exhausted relief that came with the ending of the week. Gillian had been 'on call' to the students until after 11 pm every night of the week. (Our days began promptly at 9.30 am. There were *no* excuses for late attendance). Lamblike to her example, I too tried to offer my critical services to a boisterous party of sixteen sixteen-year-old English students, for whom the words 'enough', 'tiredness', and 'sleep' did not seem to appear in any dictionary. Home again after the rail journey from Hebden to south Wales, I remained stupefied for days. And yet exhilarated. After all, I had done it. (Actually Gillian had done most of it). I had tutored a poetry course. I who was still learning to write my own poetry.

Since then hopefully, I have developed a little more stamina, (although still apprenticed in the fiendish mysteries of verse,) but what remains is an overwhelming impression of the energy of Gillian Clarke, and her genuine solicitude, not shared, let us be frank, by every writing tutor in the world, for the outpourings and the morale of her course members.

And because of the quality of that care, Gillian finds it reciprocated. After all, it was she who was responsible for attracting members to the inaugural course at Tŷ Newydd, Llanystumdwy. Thus the twelve who gathered in north Wales, in April 1990, had come, not only to support the launch of a writers' centre (a hugely ambitious undertaking), but to experience a week in the company of someone who had become established by that date as perhaps the most 'successful' (if these things can be measured in such a way) writing tutor in the UK. Gillian's 'old hands' included Mavis Carter, whose dewy, dark green Gordon's, ritually produced and lovingly, lingeringly unscrewed at one minute past six every evening, sun over the yardarm or not, provided a not unspiritual restorative for flagging course members.

Once again I served as co-tutor, but this time I was present at the birth of what has become a remarkable institution in Wales. (Tŷ Newydd, because of the community rootedness of its administrators, provides memorable social as well as cultural experiences. And not least of its importance is that it introduces the Welsh language as a natural, livng language to those who might not know of its existence. Equally of note, it

brings together people from north and south Wales—
historically rather a rare occurrence and today still unusual.) I
hovered on the fringes, listening, learning, stealing ideas,
cadging refills of the well-chilled juniper juice from the
generous Mavis. Llŷn was pretty unfamiliar to me also. After
all, the Welsh are poor travellers, and if they do move, tend
to get lost. But Gillian Clarke helped bring the stranger into
the fold.

Since that time, Gillian as tutor has explored other
intriguing possibilities, including the combinations of
mountaineering and poetry, and art and print-making with
poetry. She has also been endlessly busy in schools across the
UK. Thus perhaps more than most writers, Gillian Clarke
understands the dangers of too intensive a workload 'teaching'
poetry in schools and centres such as Tŷ Newydd or Lumb
Bank. Indeed, I believe that the constant demands of the
educational world have prevented Gillian Clarke's writing
from developing as it should. This is a matter that has
concerned me for some time.

Today all editors of UK poetry magazines recognize the
'workshop poem'. And all tutors, if they are writers,
understand the dangers to their own work inherent in too
arduous a programme of tutoring.

There are those, inevitably, who mock the very business of
creative tutoring in the arts, claiming that talent cannot be
instructed upon, and is in the gift of Heaven or Hell. Indeed,
a creative writing tutor might agree that the sum of a
lifetime's dedicated endeavour might merely be the congeries
of inadequate texts that clog the postboxes of editors and
publishers. But this would be too cynical. Writers-as-tutors
are not concerned with making the literary fortunes or
reputations of their charges. What they are paid
unhandsomely to do is encourage the confidence of the
imagination and suggest ways in which its overwhelming
powers might be employed in art. Above all, tutors must be,
to overwork two fashionable words, 'empowerers' and

41

'enablers'. But not in the social sense which often applies to those terms. Creative writing tutors atttempt to enable and empower the imaginative process. They are (or should be) the transmitters of encouragement, the generators of artistic energy.

All these roles Gillian Clarke fulfils. And in a world of increasing global uniformity, where the richness of cultural and ecological diversity is regarded as a handicap to corporate expansion and profit, and where every aspect of our lives has been influenced by the hallucinogens of consumerism, the imagination is the last redoubt.

Gillian Clarke's career as a creative writing tutor has been dedicated to illustrating how vital the exercise of that imagination is to the real quality of life. It has been rare and rewarding work.

Ahead
(At Lumb Bank with Gillian Clarke)

After rain this mountain
Leaks like a colander.
Somewhere there's a current drumming
Or the oak vanes of a waterwheel,
Then out of the valley
Blue-vested Halifax Harriers
Startling as kingfishers
Are scittering past.

I watch the faces of Saturday
Athletes unmovable on some
Target of chimney or tree,
And for a moment must stand
In the millrace of their breath
As a stone those bodies break around.

And they pass with elbows
Crooked neatly as dancers,
The shine of speed in sweat-gashed eyes.
Whatever's ahead is reeling
Them in on trajectories
They would not wish to deflect,
While leaping from the crevices
Each spate of water mingles in one yarn.

Robert Minhinnick
(poem taken from *Singing Brink*, Arvon Press, 1987)

43

Staying to mind things:
Gillian Clarke's early poetry[1]

The account any poet chooses to offer of himself is always fascinating and significant; and in our time all the more so, perhaps, when that self is a herself. In her poem 'Llŷr', Gillian Clarke traces her origins as a poet back to Stratford. There, in what elsewhere she has called one of Shakespeare's 'father-daughter plays',[2] she was 'taught the significance of little words'.[3] And what significance they turned out to have. With its tragic demonstration of how dangerous it may be for woman, in a man's world, either to speak or to remain silent, and its painfully glorious demonstration of the way the English language may eloquently appropriate and distort indigenous Welsh materials, *King Lear* provided the ten-year-old Clarke with an 'object lesson' that was eventually to set her up for life. Almost fifty years later she was to find in writings such as Eavan Boland's remarkable *Object Lessons* powerful confirmation of central aspects of her own early history as a woman poet. 'As I read the poems of the [Irish] tradition,' wrote Boland, 'it could often seem to me that I was entering a beautiful and perilous world filled with my own silence'.[4] But long before reading words such as these, Clarke had had to find ways of empowering herself to write; ways of granting herself permission to be a poet; ways of coming to understand that 'for me poetry is a rhythmic way of thinking, but it is a thought informed by the heart, informed by the body, informed by the whole self and the whole life lived, so that being a woman and being Welsh are inescapably expressed in the art of poetry.'[5]

Absent from the poem 'Llŷr' is the aunt who, Clarke subsequently explained in an essay, had actually taken the ten-year-old on that fateful outing. Written out of the text, shouldered verbally aside by Shakespeare, Lear, Laughton, and Olivier, that aunt seems now to stand for the female self that Clarke eventually discovered needed to be 'outed'. Thus identified, Auntie Phyllis (to give her her real name) may also conveniently stand for the need to relocate the sources of poetry in the traditional domain of the female. In a world where poetry is Shakespeare and therefore male, Shakespeare's very language nevertheless runs 'like a nursery rhythm' in Gillian Clarke's head.

In the magnificent concluding peroration of *A Room of One's Own*, Virginia Woolf urges women to realise that '[Shakespeare's dead sister] lives in you and in me, and in many other women who are not here tonight, for they are washing up the dishes and putting the children to bed.'[6] Gillian Clarke is making an analogous point when she takes Shakespeare back to his nursery, and to hers, describing her genesis as a poet in the process. As she has explained, her own love-affair with language began with nursery rhymes, playground games, biblical language, and Welsh hymns (*HPW*, 124). And before ever she encountered Lear or Cordelia (and how intricately the one name there echoes and recasts the other), she had already identified with Branwen, the daughter of Lear's prototype, the Welsh king Llŷr. Moreover, in another example of breaking the male monolopy over the creative imagination, Clarke recalls how, on first hearing the phrase 'The isle is full of noises' spoken on stage, she recognised it as arising from, and applying to, her own wartime experience as a child:

> My father's radio was the voice of the radio-teller. Later, when I was ten, I was to hear Shakespeare's words, and would at once know they were describing the 'sounds and sweet airs' of Fforest. It was not difficult to imagine my grandmother's farm as an isle full of noises, cut off by the sea, poor roads, weather and the family from bombs, sirens and air raids, though not from the rumours of war. Life into language equals fiction. (*HPW*, 124)

Her grandmother's farm thus becomes the setting for *The Tempest*, with Clarke implicitly acting Prospero on her 'island'.

45

In admitting that she has been writing such '"fiction" . . . all my life', Clarke is of course tacitly admitting that she has always been a poet. But hers was a gradual and phased awakening to that fact, since her society neglected to offer her the means to authentic self-recognition. Poetry seemed largely the preserve of the male, and such was the manifest authority of the great masters whose work she studied while reading English at University College, Cardiff, that Clarke was into her thirties before she found the confidence to publish her work.

True, she had kept a diary since she was fifteen, a form of writing that was wellsuited to her early life as young wife and as mother to three children whose needs monopolised her attention. But then in 1970-71 she stumbled upon a new identity, and with it she entered upon a new life, almost unawares:

> I threw my first poems in the bin because I was unaware they were poems. I suppose it was because I hadn't read anything in print that was like what I was writing. I think we all need models, and I was both Welsh and a woman. The world wasn't very interested in either. Have you noticed how late in their careers women get published? Both Ruth Bidgood and Jean Earle, whose work I like, were published late in their lives. I read *Poetry Wales*, and I saw things there that spoke to half of me, the Welsh part. It would never have occurred to me to send work to London. My former husband posted some poems off to *Poetry Wales* because I had said 'I could write as well as this.' Meic Stephens, the editor at that time, wrote back accepting them.[7]

This simple statement is dense with quiet details that turn it into the most poignant of parables about the development of Welsh women's writing. Poetry's failure to recognise itself, in the absence of any objective confirmation of its status; a woman's dependence on men for identity and opportunity; these and other features of the case make it troublingly exemplary.

Joseph Conrad chose a striking remark by Novalis as epigraph to *Lord Jim*: 'It is certain any conviction gains infinitely the moment another soul will believe in it.' *Poetry Wales*, a magazine founded by Meic Stephens in 1965, partly in order to allow English-language poets to contribute to the revitalised nationalist culture of the period, helped provide Welsh poets with self-belief and thus sponsored an important new generation of Welsh writers. It so happens that the author of the first poem in the first issue was Alison Bielski, and such writers as Ruth Bidgood and Sally Roberts [Jones] (the only woman featured in Bryn Griffiths' important 1967 anthology *Welsh Voices*) also figured prominently in the early numbers, but the contributors were preponderantly male, consistent with the gender profile of the literary culture of the period. Beginning with Gillian Clarke's significant appearance in 1970, however, a change began to occur. And just as it is appropriate that Meic Stephens, the mover and shaker of the poetry scene in Wales during the later sixties, should (with Sam Adams) have acted as male midwife to this new development, so is it appropriate that Roland Mathias, a major influence on the ideological restructuring of Anglo-Welsh literature in the postwar period, should have so readily and rapidly provided Gillian Clarke (first as contributor and then as editor) with the opportunity of redesigning *The Anglo-Welsh Review*. Jeremy Hooker, a poet and critic himself at that time emerging as an important new talent on the Anglo-Welsh scene, was another who was quick to recognize Clarke's potential. And in choosing four of her poems for his *Poems '71* volume he set a pattern to be followed for several years by his successors as selectors of the best poems to have appeared in Wales.

By (presumably) a coincidence, the first poem Gillian Clarke ever published in *Poetry Wales* was about the coming alive of a dead self.[8] 'Beech Buds' likens the experience to the putting of dry, bare twigs in water: 'From the hard,/Brittle wood came tenderness and life, numerous/Damp, green

47

butterflies, transparently veined,/Opening like a tree that is alive.' It also so happens that, with its naively unguarded exclamations ('I feel so happy'), its conspicuous evidence of delicate sensibility, and its implicit representation of the female self as dependent on male sustenance, the poem could have been read by males as reassuringly, stereotypically, 'feminine'! A similar reassurance seems to radiate from 'Nightride' and 'Sailing', with their emphasis respectively on warmly protective and anxious maternal care.

In its immediate difference, though, a fourth poem from that first set, 'The Fox', not only suggests a much more edgy and self-troubled sensibility than may previously have been apparent but also has the power to persuade us to re-read those other poems with an altogether less complacent eye. It is the kind and the quality of the sensuous writing in these poems that now comes into startling focus. A child's head is seen as 'nodding on its stalk' in 'Nightride'; in 'Beech Buds' twigs dipped in water produce 'bubbles/Of silver against the light'; and in 'The Fox', a hill is set 'flying free and horizontal from the plane of symmetry.' In such lines the senses are as it were given their head; that is, they are granted a mind, and with it a life, of their own. They set us free to feel how we come to both ripeness and vulnerability in our small children; how the very air we breathe may have aesthetic as well as functional qualities; how a transgressive wildness may be inhering in the most solidly familiar mass and matter.

Yet, as early as these 'first' poems, Clarke ironically lays herself open to the charge of deriving her poetry from influential contemporary male models. So, in its fascination with the violent convergence of life and death as expressed through the configuration of ewes giving bloody birth, little silver skulls smeared with gore, a fox hanged red and dead from a tree, Gillian Clarke seems to be trespassing on the Gothic pastoral territory of Ted Hughes. But although at this early stage Clarke's personal touch is by no means sure ('the lambs/Leapt away round the hill'), there is nevertheless already a sense not of mere imitation but of a conversation between poets that is also a conversation between genders. 'The Fox' is a poem not only by a woman but also about the ambivalence of female 'nature'. The ewe and her lambs is contrasted not with the predatory 'fox' (of the deliberately misleading title) but with the vixen, in whose violent death may be seen the full ambivalence of her nature—her warm flaming beauty, her role as provider of both milk *and* raw meat for her young, her dual aspect of killer and victim. Similarly, in another poem, 'Birth', the Hughes-like registering of the sticky, messy physicality of the process of calving ('Hot and slippery, the scalding/Baby came') is offset by a human mother's empathy with the cow. This is registered both through the sensual recall of the erotic physiology of the newly maternalised body ('I could feel the soft sucking/ Of the new-born, the tugging pleasure/Of bruised reordering, the signal/Of milk's incoming tide') and through the diffusion of the birthing experience throughout the landscape ('The light flowed out leaving stars/And clarity'). The latter involves a strategy of refiguring the body as world, a strategy which has traditionally been central to male love poetry but which has drawn upon uniquely female experience only in recent decades.

That Hughes was a very important presence in the mind of the young Gillian Clarke is not, of course, to be disputed. So, too, undoubtedly was Seamus Heaney, whose significance for her—again so frequently diminished and distorted in easy prattle about 'influence'—she has subtly explained:

A poet like Seamus Heaney has a tremendously feminine sensibility, and because Seamus Heaney is such an extremely good poet, he admitted possibilities that weren't there before, which women are now exploring. To put it another way, more women began to be published, which enabled us to see a poet like Seamus Heaney. I wonder whether he would have been so well received by an earlier generation, when feminine values were less noticed and admired. (*UI*, 28-9)

It is the mutuality of the indebtedness that is fruitfully insisted upon here, and indeed Clarke demonstrates exactly what she means in the accomplished early poem 'Lunchtime Lecture', clearly an interesting variant on Heaney's celebrated Bog Queen poems. (Although it is interesting to note that an English translation of 'Geneth Ifanc' ['Young Girl'], Waldo Williams' familiar Welsh-language poem about the feelings of kinship awakened in him by the 'stone skeleton' from the Iron Age, was printed directly following Clarke's first poems in *Poetry Wales*.) The moment of her encounter with the skeleton of a young female from the second or third millennium BC at once reproduces, in an entirely different key and setting, Heaney's mental exhumation of a long buried life, and claims a kind of priority over it, since there is between Clarke and her 'subject' an intuitive understanding, based on shared gender experience, to which he can lay no claim: 'She's a tree in winter, . . . /I, at some other season, . . . /We stare at each other, dark into sightless/Dark.'[9] It is as if Clarke had been admitted by Heaney into a world of experience which was already hers by right, and which her sex had in the first instance made available to him.

In fact, the supportive presence of pioneering women writers is as palpable in Clarke's early texts as is the 'influence' of her prominent male contemporaries. Sylvia Plath's 'Morning Song', the opening poem in *Ariel* (1965), seems in some ways to foreshadow, and in a sense to make possible, the poem 'Baby Sitting', with which Clarke's first collection, *Snow on the Mountain* (1971), opens. Except, of course, that Plath's distinguishing note of raw self-exposure is missing from Clarke's altogether more gentle and composed poem of self-knowledge. That difference seems to determine, as much as to be determined by, their respective choice of subject, with Plath owning up to her resentful attachments to her selfishly demanding brat of a baby that seems like a mere monstrous automaton of need, and Clarke, markedly less daring, reflecting guiltily on her cold, nervous imperviousness to the blind demands of a baby that is not her own. But elsewhere in *Snow on the Mountain* she, too, probes as deep as the vein of anger and resentment that can run through maternal love. In 'Catrin' she explores, in her perhaps too conciliatory way, the struggle for separateness that locks mother and teenage daughter into a newly intense relationship.

Relationships are, in fact, at the heart (in every sense) of Clarke's early poetry. Indeed, in three of the quartet of poems she originally published in *Poetry Wales* she defines herself in terms of her relationship with somebody else. Moreover, her coming into new being, as described in 'Beech Buds', is imaged as issuing directly from an immersion of self in another's 'brightness'. Such a generously joyous image of powerless indebtedness seems strikingly un-masculine, and seems, further, to anticipate that sense of female selfhood, and that view of female writing, that Gillian Clarke was later to expound in her prose. 'Men', she wrote in an important essay in the Bloodaxe catalogue, 'often observe themselves in poems. They cast themselves into roles. It is called "being objective". Craig Raine sees himself as Shakespeare in one poem. Seamus Heaney sees himself as Wordsworth. Less famously, men see themselves as fathers, sons, lovers, and their poems are often written from that objective, observed viewpoint.' By contrast, she goes on to argue, 'Women often move halfway into a role, the transition incomplete and felt rather than seen . . . Is it that women spend their lives in uncertainty, never quite either the hunter-gatherer or the madonna-mistress? Certainly they show a markedly greater interest in the detail and subtlety of relationships'.[11]

The quartet of poems in *Poetry Wales* that signalled Gillian Clarke's arrival on the scene did not for some reason include 'The Sundial', the poem (her first for many years) that really marked the genesis of her poetry, and which she later selected to be the title-poem of her second (though first substantial) collection of poems. Recording a day spent caring for her sick

51

youngest child, this 'relationship' poem typifies several important aspects of Clarke's early poetry.

It is a domestic piece, thus adumbrating one of the basic tenets of that female (as opposed to feminist) poetics that Clarke began shortly later to construct, in piecemeal fashion, through her occasional writings. In an *Anglo-Welsh Review* editorial published in 1979 she argued that 'the likeliest subjects of female writing [are] the domestic and familiar, and the way of looking at relationships, places, objects, and society that is inclined to be minutely perceptive and detailed. It is an under-valued perception and "domestic" and "familiar" are too frequently taken to be derogatory words. The "domus" is one of our society's most unheard messages, powerhouse as that place is for every emerging adult.'[12] Elsewhere she has retrospectively dubbed these early poems 'indoorscapes', indicating they were 'artlessly, instinctively written, and that mood ended with publication.'[13] She has also drawn attention to their 'presentness', that is their preoccupation with the pressing, though passing, concerns of the invariably crowded domestic moment, a feature particularly evident in a poem that starts, as does 'The Sundial', 'Owain was ill today' (*S*,11) and a characteristic that may betray the continuity between these early attempts at poetry and her already well established practice of keeping a diary of the day's events.

A less immediately evident, but ultimately perhaps more significant, aspect of the poem is its manner of investigating the workings of the imagination. The feverish boy has been delirious during the night, 'shouting of lions/In the sleepless heat.' Now, still 'slightly/Trembling with fever', he patiently fashions a sundial out of paper, a stick, and some stones, in order to calculate 'the mathematics of sunshine.' His mother is struck by his newfound, silent, adult-like concentration: 'he found/Deliberation, and the slow finger/Of light, quieter than night lions.' (*S*, 11) This aspect of the poem—its focussing on a moment when the boy begins to probe for hidden

52

patterns of energy and to trace invisible rhythms of light—becomes much more apparent when it is read in the context of the other poems in *Snow on the Mountain*, the little booklet of poems by Clarke that was published as Number Five of the *Triskel Poets* series in 1971.

The title-poem of that collection is itself full of what, on the analogy of 'The Sundial', one might call 'the mathematics of snow'. In other words, it shows how new angles on reality emerge as one struggles to find one's bearings in a world rendered strange, blankly elemental, and apparently featureless by snow. So the family, out to clamber up the snow-covered heights of the hills around Machen, fixes its attention on a bird: 'A crow cut a clean line/Across the hill, which we grasped as a rope/To pull us up the pale diagonal.'[14] This heightened attention to, and trust in, the draught-manship and texture of the visible is deeply characteristic of a poet one of whose greatest loves is the visual arts. And such a passion for form and colour is everywhere evident in her work—so in the wake of a vixen's death all the reds in a day that had begun 'warm with colour' grow cold; and, elsewhere, a cow standing up creates the chiaroscuro effect of 'cool/Flanks like white flowers in the dark.' (*SM*, 22) But it is not only that Clarke is a painterly poet; she is also a poet for whom language itself is a thickly sensuous medium, a medium to the enchantment of which one needs almost languorously to submit, so that it can then be intuitively worked, as a painter works paint, until unexpected forms of meaning seem miraculously to appear. As she has explained, 'After pen and paper, the beauty of the empty cleanness, there is energy. It sets me thinking. I try the paper to see what the words will do. It must be like drawing . . . try the line, see what happens.'[15] The echo of Paul Klee's celebrated description of drawing as taking a line for a walk is unmistakable here.

The new discoveries that come only through the suspension of conventional rational intelligence and its spuriously authoritative categories of description have been a constant preoccupation of Clarke's over the years. Of late she has, for instance, confessed her attraction to the 'new nature poems [which] are scientific rather than lyrical, concerned but not romantic. They aim to match the precision of metaphor and word-patterns to the clarity of the fact. They relish the patterning of things, the connections between the worlds of nature and ideas.' (*OSL*, 292) The analogy with her own work is evident, except that her means of achieving the same ends are somewhat different. She has always on the one hand been drawn to mythopoeic descriptions, whose devastating power to re-form reality she has repeatedly distinguished from arbitrary fantasy (her son's night-lions), while on the other being attracted to rhythms and patterns (of both sound and perception) that involve profound realignments of reason.

So 'Community', the concluding poem in *Snow on the Mountain*, appropriately speaks of how, in company, 'one can stand aside and watch/The spatial movement, understanding/ Edge forward, falter and change/Form.' (*SM*, 30) Elsewhere in the collection, too, deepening understanding is troped in terms of forms described in space. 'Lines' centres on the way a scene, and with it the day, is intersected diagonally by the wavering edge of a washing line, which comes to represent 'That wound of the divided/Mind' (*SM*, 20). 'Waterfall' is about following the path that 'led me under the fall to feel/The arc of the river and the mountain's exact/Weight; the roar of rain and lapwings/Leaving; water-beat, heart-fall in accord' (*SM*, 14). And already embryonically apparent in these early poems is 'that sense of moving from one image to another as if searching, as if not fully committed to a role, the metaphor not seen but felt.' (*H-G*, 20). So memories of giving birth register as a feeling of 'satisfaction/Fall[ing] like a clean sheet around me' (*SM*, 22), and the head of a dead curlew chick 'Loll[s] from the snapped stem of its neck/Like the hung clock of a dandelion/Wasting its seed.' (*SM*, 24)

Remarks such as the above about images and metaphors are really fragments of Gillian Clarke's female poetics, a poetics, grounded in her developing understanding of female experience, upon which she has been unsystematically at work virtually since she began to publish her poems. So, for instance, her own early awareness of having constantly to shift roles from wife to mother to housewife to teacher to editor to poet underlies her emphasis on the provisional, exploratory, and tentative nature of the stances and images women tend fluidly to produce in their writings: such, she suggests, is also the magically unpredictable and unstable world which the *Mabinogion* conjures up for us. This has further led her to reflect on the subversively shifting sense of perspective and scale that a woman's constantly changing role, or theatre of operations, entails. For Clarke, therefore, a woman is naturally possessed of a power to tilt the world off its familar axis, that convulsive power of the artistic imagination that has traditionally been figured through stories of giants like Bendigeidfran. Similarly, her association of poetry with energies and rhythms of intuition that are anterior to consciousness relates in part to her theory of female psychological development:

> The girl-child often has an early advantage in language skills, is likely to talk earlier, to learn to read sooner than a boy and to prefer imaginative literature. Words store memory. 'Nothing is until it has a word.' ('Llŷr') Women oftener record memories of babyhood than men and thus draw more deeply on the first physical, animal sensations of infancy, where body and mind are single, fact and imagination indivisible. It is not that men never share this characteristic, as Heaney proves, but that it is rarer in men, and might even be said to be commonplace in women. (*OSL*, 288)

The ascertainable truth of this statement probably matters less than its capacity, as belief or modern myth, to enable and to empower women to write. Indeed, Clarke's own writing, at first womanly only in fairly superficial though significant ways, could be said to have been deepened and enriched through that continuing exploration of female identity she has undertaken primarily in her poetry and secondarily in her complementary prose.

That awakening to herself as poet, which entailed new explorations of herself as woman, seems further to have involved, in Gillian Clarke's case, the beginning of a process of personal reintegration which was grounded, as it were, at Blaen Cwrt, the dilapidated farm cottage in rural west Wales that came into her possession in the early seventies. Indeed, the importance of this location is perceptively noted by Sam Adams in his Introduction to *Snow on the Mountain*, a document that is a valuable record of how Clarke's emergence as a poet was at that time viewed by individuals closely connected with it and with her:

> The revival of her creative interest in poetry coincided with the finding of a cottage in Cardiganshire where the family now spend as much time as possible. Many of her poems are about this quieter world, far removed from the suburbia of Cardiff, much more closely involved with the rhythms of the seasons. Here she observes the constantly changing patterns of nature, the integration of rural landscape, bird and beast. All this she records with superb delicacy and tact, finding in her experience of motherhood analogies for the fertility of the natural world and the pangs of birth and separation. She takes as her main themes areas of life infrequently explored in poetry and very rarely indeed illuminated with such honesty and insight—the interplay of relationships within the family, and the family observed against the background of nature.

Only very recently, with the publication not only of *The King of Britain's Daughter* but also of two important essays associated with the writing of that volume's title sequence, has it become possible to understand fully what that part of Ceredigion in which Blaen Cwrt is situated actually means to Gillian Clarke.[16] For her it represents her idyllic childhood retreat, that spot of time (to adopt, and adapt Wordsworth's celebrated phrase) where her artistic sensibility was nurtured, where she grew unawares into a writer, where the tensions between her parents (symbolised, as she has put it, by their quarrels over the Welsh language) could be magically suspended, where she felt snugly secluded and yet (thanks to her radio-engineer father) tuned in to the wavelength of the whole wild world, where the landscape was haunted and sculpted by giant imagination, and where she felt as ladied by her grandmother and nature as the boy Dylan Thomas had felt lorded at Fern Hill. Although her actual home, both as a child and later as a wife and mother, was in Cardiff, she was most really and truly at home in west Wales. As she has written, 'The fact that literature, from nursery rhyme and fairy story onwards, was so closely associated with the natural world, has played a strong part in making me a country person, not an urban one, even during the long years of my life spent in the city. Literature hallowed the natural with the supernatural. It made the stones sing. It populated the countryside with animals, seen and unseen. It made natural phenomena reverberate with mythological meaning, turned a rocking stone to a giant's apple, a rock pool to a footprint.' (*OSL*, 280)

It would be wrong to bring all these insights with which Clarke has provided us in the nineties to bear uncritically on her poetry of the seventies—wrong not least because as she has made clear it is only by painful degrees that she herself has come to understand her childhood, and its locations, in these terms. Nevertheless, to read her early poem 'Blaen Cwrt' with a judicious degree of hindsight is not only to appreciate anew the terms in which it consciously celebrates a rediscovered community with place, and a place with its own unique community, it is also to sense for the first time the unconscious feelings working like yeast and helping the phrases swell to a rich fullness of meaning.

'Blaen Cwrt', too, is a 'relationship' poem, beginning as it does by addressing an interlocutor: 'You ask how it is. I will tell you.' (*SM*, 10) And this is appropriate since the poem as a whole is about 'relating', is indeed about a place that in an important sense really exists only in Clarke's relating to it, which in turn is inscribed in her relating of it. Equally, it exists only as a place held in common—the stress throughout is on the first person plural, the language is one of encounter ('Holding a thick root/I press my bucket through the surface/ Of the water'), the similes are social connectives ('Our fingers curl on/Enamel mugs of tea, like ploughmen'), the syntax is a homogenizing device ('All is ochre and earth and cloud-green/ Nettles'), and everywhere there is the semiotics of co-existence ('Some of the smoke/Rises against the ploughed, brown field/As a sign to our neighbours in the/Four folds of the valley that we are in'). Integration of the self, and simultaneous integration into a community of people and nature, are the poem's implicit themes, made explicit in the concluding lines:

> It has all the first
> Necessities for a high standard
> Of civilised living: silence inside
> A circle of sound, water and fire,
> Light on uncountable miles of mountain
> From a big, unpredictable sky,
> Two rooms, waking and sleeping,
> Two languages, two centuries of past
> To ponder on, and the basic need
> To work hard in order to survive. (*SM*, 10)

Dealing, as it so obviously does, with the theme of 'belonging' —a central topos of the sixties, almost obsessively figured throughout that decade as a search for 'roots'— 'Blaen Cwrt' is in danger of appearing to be a dated product of its time. That it can still nevertheless command attention through the power and the measured dignity of its speech may be due partly to those unconscious feelings that, as Clarke has recently enabled us to see, were secretly animating her attachment to the cottage. For instance, the way these concluding lines seek to contain and pacify instability ('a big, unpredictable sky'), and their resemblance to an epithalamium —a celebration of the marriage between Wales's two cultures — acquires a poignancy when read in the light of the tensions in Clarke's early family background.

Moreover, the poem is very much a portrait of that artist Clarke had, at the time of writing, newly come to realise she was. Her visual acuity, her painterly eye for colour and texture, are abundantly evident throughout ('The stones clear in the rain/Giving their colours. It's not easy./There are no brochure blues or boiled sweet/Reds'). The point, as in several of Wordsworth's greatest poems, is that only to the patiently loving attention of one who is inward with it does this scene 'give' its colour and reveal itself as beautiful. And again like the Wordsworth of 'Michael', Clarke insists that only to those who know it well will this place entrust its history: 'The wattle and daub/Chimney hood has decayed away, slowly/Creeping to dust, chalking the slate/Floor with stories.' Moreover, by so clearly emphasising at the outset her intention to 'tell' her reader/listener not about Blaen Cwrt but literally 'how it is', Clarke is demonstrating the power of language and the authority to be a poet that is vested in her by this place. In this respect, the poem is her signature text as a writer, and specifically as a woman writer, because (in spite of my references to Wordsworth), the kind of sensuous immersion in, and receptive submission to, the ancient particularities of a landscape that is registered in 'Blaen Cwrt' is associated in Gillian Clarke's mind with a 'feminine' sensibility. Thus the poem may be read as a celebration of a feminized—and indeed feminizing—landscape, centring on the implicit demonstration that Clarke's way of moving in and setting up home is not the male's way of taking possession of a property. Rather, she tentatively feels her way, adapting herself gently to what's there, taking new shape from it, just as 'Some of the smoke seeps through the stones/Into the barn where it curls like fern/On the walls.'

When Gillian Clarke moved permanently to Blaen Cwrt in 1984 it marked a new phase in her life as woman and as writer. Her children were now grown up and she was free to accept a Welsh Arts Council sponsored writer's residency at St David's University College, Lampeter. She described this as 'a change of life . . . without fracture or disruption. It seems to me that I have turned to face the already known, to know it more profoundly.'[17] But as she also wryly noted; 'In 1978 I wrote a long poem, ("Letter from a far country") about a woman who, in the spirit of feminist rebellion, threatens to leave home and family, although in the end, seduced by memory, tradition and the ties of family life, she stays. However, as one friend has remarked, on hearing of my present adventure, "So the prophecy of 'Letter' is fulfilled."' Until the early eighties, however, Clarke continued to be circumstanced in those ways upon which she so expressively reflects in 'Letter from a Far Country'.

Broadcast as a half-hour radio poem in 1978 but not published until 1982, that work is now accepted as a landmark text in Welsh writing in English. And, most notably in her preface to the selection of her work published in *Six Women Poets*, Clarke herself has written informatively about the poem. She has explained that it was written 'easily in between 10 and 15 hours spread over five late-night sessions when my sons' drums and guitars had fallen silent for the night', and has noted that the poem is both 'a celebration of life's good things—clean sheets, the smell of baking, orderliness —with which my mother and grandmother surrounded me' and 'a small contribution towards feminist protest, a meditation on traditional woman's work written in the form of an imaginary letter, the sort of letter you write in your mind and never post.' That letter, she adds, 'is a letter from a fictitious woman to all men. The "far country" is childhood, womanhood, Wales, the beautiful country where the warriors, kings and presidents don't live, the private place where we all grow up.' More pointedly, she reveals that the poem arose out of a feeling of anger and frustration at the way 'the earth—birth, death, caring, nurturing, teaching, nursing, home-making, were in women's hands, while the world—public life, money, government, organization, judgement, war, were in the hands of men. This would, perhaps, suit us well enough, if only both kinds of work were equally valued, but we all know they are not.'[18]

In those phrases from 'Blaen Cwrt' that deliberately override the difference between men's and women's work ('Our fingers curl on/Enamel mugs of tea, like ploughmen') linger, perhaps, memories of early sex discimination such as those registered in 'Letter': 'To be out with the men, at work,/I had longed to carry their tea,/For the feminine privilege,/for the male right to the field./Even that small task made me bleed.' (*LFC*, 12-13) And just as, later in the poem, women's bleeding becomes both a painful monthly fact and a metaphor for the equivocal biological and cultural terms on which woman is granted her unique power of creativity, so 'Letter from a Far Country' proceeds by recuperating aspects of female experience that males have traditionally stigmatised, and by reconceiving forms of living and writing that had previously borne the imprint only of the male imagination. Such regenerations of form are, of course, also regenderings of form. Indeed, not only does the poem force a redefinition of the 'long poem' as a genre, revealing the inherently gendered and contingent character of its supposedly intrinsic kinds of subject-matter and structure, it is also written in a flexible, and therefore unemphatic, three-stress line that seems pointedly to stop short of the full fig of the masculine iambic pentameter!

It is also important to remember that 'Letter from a far Country' was commissioned for broadcast on radio, and that it therefore belongs to the 'genre' so famously and definitively represented in Wales by *Under Milk Wood*. The very rhythm of that work's celebrated opening— 'It is spring, moonless night in the small town, starless and bible-black'[19]—seems echoed in Clarke's 'They have gone. The silence resettles/ slowly as dust on the sunlit/surfaces of the furniture.' (*LFC*, 7) Echo, indeed, seems the operative word when writing about 'Letter'. If *Under Milk Wood* is a 'Play for Voices' then Clarke's work is a Poem for Echoes. Not only is her poem about the resonances between past and present, it repeatedly figures the imagination itself as an echo-chamber and it turns words into echoes of each other, in lines like 'the ruined warehouse where the owls stare'. (*LFC*, 9) 'Listen!', she writes, again adopting one of Dylan Thomas's favourite rhetorical strategies, 'to the starlings glistening on a March morning!' (*LFC*, 10) Yes, both Thomas and Clarke are inspired users of 'alliteration and assonance', if we must trundle out those tired terms, but the significance of the fact lies in the radically different ways in which these devices speak the minds of these

two poets so decisively divided by temperament and gender. And what is really at issue is their fundamentally opposed ways of conceiving of language.

'The poet is the father of his poem; its mother is a language; one could list poems as race horses are listed—*out of L by P*', wrote W.H. Auden, demonstrating how easily a male author betrays his gender when writing about writing.[20] But elsewhere in his essays Auden more usefully distinguishes between a poet who 'thinks of the poem he is writing as something already latent in the language which he has to reveal', and one who 'thinks of language as a plastic passive medium upon which he imposes his artistic conception.' (*SE*, 134) Too absolute though such a distinction undoubtedly is —and applicable though Auden would have it be only to 'formal' and 'free verse' poets respectively—it does help us understand Clarke's obstetric relationship to language in 'Letter from a Far Country', a relationship that is, of course, inseparable from her encouraging receptivity to the past, as that is present alike in place and in woman's ambiguously 'given' place. It is evident that, as she confessed elsewhere, 'I love to find clues in language and stories to show old complexities.'[21]

For Gillian Clarke, 'Letter from a Far Country' was in many respects a threshold poem; it marked a liminal stage in her life both as woman and as writer. On the other hand *The Sundial*—her first substantial collection of poems, published after the writing but before the publication of 'Letter'—is more of a summation of her work to that date, and a retrospective exhibition of her achievements. The volume's title is well-chosen; language throughout the book struggles to track heat and light, to catch in its sounds and cadences 'the savage roar of the trapped sun/Seeding the earth against the stop of winter' (*S*, 27). And in the concluding poems in *The Sundial* death is repeatedly viewed in this light, as in the visionary, not to say apocalyptic, last verse of 'Harvest at Mynachlog':

> We are quiet again, holding our cups
> In turn for the tilting milk, sad, hearing
> The sun roar like a rush of grain
> Engulfing all winged things that live
> One moment in the eclipsing light. (*S*, 50)

Reading some of these poems is sometimes like stepping into one of the light-storms of a painting by Turner or being caught in the energy field of one of Van Gogh's quivering canvases. Not that Clarke's imagery is all of light; she is attracted equally to the headlong liquefactions of water, seeing the river in her poem 'At Ystrad Fflur', 'rac[ing] for the south too full/of summer rain for safety.' (*S*, 22) The provenance of such writing is mixed, connecting back as it does with Romantic vitalism (in both its nineteenth-century and twentieth-century modernist forms), the hyperbolic Welsh praise tradition, and the feminist poetics of fecundity. Other aspects of that poetics are apparent when Gillian Clarke beautifully notices at Ystrad Fflur 'a river blossoming on stone'. The phrase both conveys a sense of female in relation to male (with a sidelong glance at Moses?) and suggests hard matter's hidden other self—the secret sap which runs through the veins of rock. And in this last respect it connects with the language and imagery of concavity that recurs in *The Sundial*, the caves and skulls and shells that turn some of her poems into verbal equivalents of paintings by Georgia O'Keefe, to whose work she was later to address a poem.

Several of the poems in *The Sundial* carry the signs (and stigmata) of female consciousness as characterised by Clarke in her prose writings. In her essay 'The King of Britain's Daughter' she has recalled how 'as a child I used to play a game which I called "big and little".' (*HPW*, 123) In other words she saw how a stone could become a planet and the setting sun a pebble about to drop. Grown up, she was to realise that much of woman's life involved such abrupt changes in scale, a constant movement between interior and exterior, domestic and public, family and world. No better example of the habit of imagination thus inculcated could be found than her perception, in 'Two Points of View', of the resting red combine harvester (that macho machine) as standing 'still and powerful/As a ladybird resting between flight' (*S*, 46), or of her Blakean vision (yes, men can see this way too, as she would readily admit) of the curlew:

> She dips her bill in the rim of the sea.
> Her beak is the elipse
> of a world much smaller
> than that far section of the sea's
> circumference. (*S*, 36)

Another of the qualities of her female vision is apparent in 'In Pisgah Graveyard', where 'The warmth tumbles here like a giant sun/Flower dying and full of glossy seed.' (*S*, 27) There, not unlike Virginia Woolf, she demonstrates such a sensitivity to atmosphere (of places or relationships) that it is as if she possessed the poetic equivalent of a psychic's gift for perceiving 'aura' or as if she could feel the amniotic fluid of life.

'In Pisgah Graveyard' is in part an elegy for Dewi Emrys, that most maverick of Welsh-language poets of the twentieth-century. There, next to 'a poet's grave that tidies his wild life', she feels a deep affinity with one whose passion for language was so unbridled:

> This roughest stone of all, a sand-stone pod
> Bursting with words, is Dewi Emrys's grave.
> And all around the living corn concedes
> Fecundity to him. (*S*, 27)

In these images, so suggestively bisexual in nature, can be sensed a generous acknowledgement of indebtedness to, and kinship with, the male poets of Wales's past. This bond, which is also a double bind, closely resembles those feelings towards the male writers of Ireland that Eavan Boland so carefully and caringly expresses in *Object Lessons*:

> As I read the poems of the tradition, it could often seem to me that I was entering a beautiful and perilous world filled with my own silence. As I struggled to become my own subject—in poems I could hardly write and in a literary tradition which blurred the feminine and the national—these poems were enabling and illuminating. As a woman I felt some mute and anxious kinship with those erotic subjects which were appropriated; as a poet I felt confirmed by the very powers of expression which appropriated them. (*OL*, 237-238)

Several poems in *The Sundial* implicitly explore Clarke's place in the male-voice chorus of Welsh poetry. In 'Dyddgu Replies to Dafydd' she enables the mute object of the praise of Wales's greatest poet to become a speaking subject, and she thus empowers a woman to speak her own differently erotic love poem, to yearn for 'when the wind whitens the tender/underbelly of the March grass/thick as pillows under the oaks.' (*S*, 21) And in the companion poem 'At Ystrad Fflur' Gillian Clarke quietly claims, in the name of her female self, not only the place where Dafydd ap Gwilym is buried but also the traditions of praise poetry and *canu bro* which had previously been virtually a Welsh male preserve. In her poem the landscape becomes vividly female in body, culminating in a sensation of how 'desire runs//Like sparks in stubble through the memory/of the place, and a yellow mustard field/is a sheet of flame in the heart.' (*S*, 23) It is almost as if it has taken a woman to recognise, and in that sense fully to awaken, the riotous 'desire' that is pent-up in this location, that latent passion which is the true legacy of Dafydd ap Gwilym, and which is the hidden blazon of puritanically and politically oppressed Wales.

Of course, Gillian Clarke's poetry in *The Sundial* is not always so startlingly and convincingly vivid. Her poetics of deliquescence and of liquefaction, her extravagantly sensuous language, and the ringing diapason of her affirmations can sometimes seem altogether too lush and luscious. And she herself put her finger on the dangers and difficulties inherent in her early practice in an uncharacteristically impatient review of *Conundrum*, Jan Morris's book about changing sex. While emphasising (perhaps too uncritically for her own good as a poet) that 'to be female is to live a woman's life, an essentially seasonal, physical, rhythmic, body-conscious life from an early age', she also properly objects to Morris's sentimental view of the female nature: 'I must insist that we come good, bad and indifferent, placid or passionate, gentle or fierce, as men do.'[22] What one sometimes feels the want of in *The Sundial* is precisely such a full mediation, through the medium of poetry, of woman's complex fate, her incorrigibly human, as well as gendered, nature.

Nevertheless, the abiding impression left from reading

Gillian Clarke's early poetry is one of exhilaration at the headlong, head (and body) strong energy of its innovativeness. She was to go on, of course, to a new phase which also amounted in her case to a new life, and in the process she not only consolidated her talent but also developed and extended it. But there can still be felt in her early writing all the unrepeatable vigour of the adventure and excitement of self-discovery. It was then that self-awakening was achieved by 'shak[ing] words awake', and that poetry first became for her 'an unconscious act of revelation.'[23] And behind that whole process lay the determination, as she put it in 'Letter from a Far Country', to be—both as woman and as poet, but in such very different senses—the girl who 'stays. To mind things.' (*LFC*, 8)

M Wynn Thomas

[1] I am very grateful to my postgraduate student, Mrs Diane Green, for providing me with a bibliography of Gillian Clarke's writings and xeroxes of several of the more inaccessible items.

[2] 'The King of Britain's Daughter', in Tony Curtis, ed., *How Poets Work* (Bridgend: Seren, 1996), 122-126. (Hereafter *HPW*.)

[3] *Letter from a Far Country* (Manchester: Carcanet, 1982), 27. (Hereafter *LFC*.)

[4] Eavan Boland, *Object Lessons: the life of the woman and the poet in our time* (Manchester: Carcanet, 1995. Quotations from the London: Vintage, 1996 edition, 232. (Hereafter *OL*.) I am grateful to my wife, Karen Thomas, for bringing this volume to my attention.

[5] 'Beginning with Bendigeidfran', in Jane Aaron, Teresa Rees, Sandra Betts, Moira Vincentelli, eds., *Our Sisters' Land* (Cardiff: University of Wales Press, 1994), 287-293. (Hereafter *OSL*.)

[6] Virginia Woolf, *A Room of One's Own*, ed., Morag Shiach (Oxford: Oxford University Press, World's Classics, 1992), 148.

[7] 'Interview with Gillian Clarke', in David T. Lloyd, ed., *The Urgency of Identity: Contemporary English-Language Poetry From Wales* (Evanston, Illinois: Northwestern University Press, 1994), 29. (Hereafter *UI*.)

[8] Gillian Clarke's poetry first appeared in *Poetry Wales* 6:1 (1970), 18-20.

[9] 'Lunchtime Lecture', *The Sundial* (Llandysul: Gomer, 1978), 13. (Hereafter *S*.)

[10] 'Morning Song', *Ariel* (London: Faber, 1965; quotations from Faber, 1968 edition), 11.

[11] 'Hunter-gatherer or madonna mistress?', *Bloodaxe Catalogue, 1986-7*, 20. (Hereafter *H-G.*)

[12] Editorial, *The Anglo-Welsh Review* (1979).

[13] Introduction to her own work, in Meic Stephens, ed., *The Bright Field: An Anthology of Contemporary Poetry From Wales* (Manchester: Carcanet, 1991), 54. (Hereafter *BF.*)

[14] 'Snow on the Mountain', in *Snow on the Mountain* (Swansea and Llandybie: Christopher Davies, 1971. The Triskel Poets Series, Number Five), 18. (Hereafter *SM.*)

[15] Interview with Gillian Clarke, in Susan Butler, ed., *Common Ground: Poets in a Welsh Landscape* (Bridgend: Poetry Wales Press, 1985), 198. (Hereafter *CG.*)

[16] The two essays are 'Beginning with Bendigeidfran', and 'The King of Britain's Daughter' (see above).

[17] 'In Literary Residence', *Llais Llyfrau/Book News From Wales* (1984).

[18] 'Gillian Clarke: the Poet's Introduction', in Judith Kinsman, ed., *Six Women Poets* (Oxford: Oxford University Press, 1992), 1.

[19] *Under Milk Wood*, ed., Daniel Jones (London: Dent, Everyman edition, 1992), 1. I have, of course, omitted the opening line: 'To begin at the beginning.'

[20] 'D.H. Lawrence', in W.H. Auden, *Selected Essays* (London: Faber, 1964), 31. (Hereafter *SE.*)

[21] '*Letting in the Rumour*: a letter from a far country, by Gillian Clarke', *Poetry Book Society Bulletin*: 141 (1989), 14.

[22] Review of Jan Morris, *Conundrum*, in *The Anglo-Welsh Review*: 53 (1974), 259.

[23] The phrases are taken from 'Writer's Diary', *Llais Llyfrau/Book News From Wales* (Spring, 1993), 4.

Manafon

Have I had to wait
all this time to discover
its meaning—that rectory,
mahogany of a piano
the light played on? What
it was saying to the unasked
question was: '*The* answer
is here'. The woman was right;
she knew it, the truth china
can tell in a cool pantry;
the web happiness can weave
that catches nothing but the dew's
years. The one flight over
that valley was that
of the wild geese. The river's
teeth chattered but not
with the cold. The woman tended
a wood fire against my return
from my wanderings, a silent entreaty
to me to cease my bullying
of the horizon. There was a dream
she kept under her pillow
that has become my nightmare.
It was the unrecognised conflict
between two nations, the one happy
in the territory it had gained,
determined to keep it; the other
with the thought he could kiss the feet
of the Welsh rainbow. I was shown
the fact: a people with a language
and an inheritance for sale;
their skies noisy with armed aircraft,
their highways sluices for their neighbours'
discharge. If I wet my feet

it was in seas radiant but not with well-being.
I retire at night beneath stars
that have gone out. I stand
with my friends at a cross-road
where there is no choice. No matter;
that nightmare is a steed I am
content to ride so it return
with me here among countrywomen
whose welcome is warm at the grave's edge.
It is a different truth, a different
love I have come to, but one
I share with that afflicted remnant
as we go down, inalienable to our defeat.

R. S. Thomas

Tŷ Newydd

It all started in August, 1989, when Gillian Clarke and Meic Stephens, then Literature Director of the Welsh Arts Council, visited Tŷ Newydd and sensed that they had found the place they had been looking for. They wanted a writers' centre, modelled on the Arvon centres, which would be for Wales. It would nurture and encourage Welsh writers of all ages, at all levels and from all backgrounds. It would be a place which would encourage reading and the appreciation of literature and be a place that every Welsh writer could feel was theirs. It would be a house where writers could come together, a place for retreat, a place that provided work, a network and a framework and somewhere that would inspire, give confidence and open doors. Gillian, who had tutored so often at the Arvon Foundation houses at Lumb Bank and Totleigh Barton, was evangelical about the value of such a place for the writers of Wales, and it was her passion and hard campaigning that had persuaded the Arts Council to support the idea.

Tŷ Newydd, a house dating back to the sixteenth century, is a hotch-potch of architecture. This gives it its charm. The front is Queen Anne, imposing and elegant, yet at night, with the lights on it is a doll's house, warm and homely. It is hard to believe that this belongs to the same house as the turrets, pillars, assortments of chimneys and windows which are on the south-facing part of the house. The interior is made up of a similar jumble of styles and rooms. There are large elegant rooms and small cosy rooms. There is the library, with its bay window overlooking the gardens to the sea and mountains, like a ship on a calm sea. And there are the nooks and the crannies; ideal spaces to creep away into in order to write, or think, or read, or play hide-and-seek. This house has grown organically over the centuries, generations adding on bits as they needed. Lloyd George in the 1940s commissioned Sir Clough Williams-Ellis to make substantial alterations and all this this must contribute to the feeling of informality, the feeling that this a house where people come first. For it is a house that welcomes you in and is loath to let you go.

It was very quickly decided in that autumn in 1989 that Tŷ Newydd was to change from being a language and study centre, privately run, into a writers' centre run by the Taliesin Trust, a body which would be made up of individuals committed to the idea of a residential writers' centre for Wales. It was a frantic time, trying to get Tŷ Newydd ready for the first course at Easter. The commitment to the project, however, was overwhelming. Writers throughout Wales sent money, books and offers of help. It was a good time, too, full of optimism and goodwill, as well as of panic.

I have snapshot memories of that time: a volunteer painting himself as well as the ceiling, the newspaper reporter, stilletoes stuck between the cobbles, the blowsy rhodedendrons we cut to adorn the house and hide the patches we had forgotten to paint. I remember the doubts I had too. There were to be no more balmy summer evenings catching moths in the garden, no more Sunday music afternoons with tea and no more jazz workshops culminating in jam sessions with only our old saucepans and buckets as a drum kit. Would the fact that it was becoming part of the establishment mean that it would lose its spontaneity, its flexibility and its charm? Time has proved that my fears were completely unfounded, but I was loath to let go physically of Tŷ Newydd at that time and the family stubbornly stayed in the downstairs of Tŷ Newydd while courses ran above us.

We survived for just over a year, sharing the garden with course members and living far too closely to every course. The catering arrangements were utter madness. Meals, except on the first evening when we ate in the hall, were prepared and eaten in the large kitchen in Hafodty, a converted outhouse, a good thirty yards from Tŷ Newydd itself. There was only one small electric cooker in there to cook for groups of up to twenty, so we also had to use 'the little kitchen', (consisting of a Baby Belling, a kettle and a sink) in the main building and then our kitchen downstairs which had a Rayburn. Menus had to be devised so that they could be cooked on trays that fitted in these tiny ovens. We would lurch between the three kitchens, trying to co-ordinate the timing of the different constituents of the meals and then run with plates of steaming food, under umbrellas when it was raining, to Hafodty, where bemused writers would be squashed round tables set diagonally across the kitchen in order to accommodate them all. This lunacy ended abruptly one day when a thick pea-souper of a fog rolled up the garden from the sea. The steaming baked potatoes that I was carrying from one building to another rolled off the tray and down the steps into the courtyard, never to be seen again. The family moved into Hafodty after that and mealtimes became more civilised if less adventurous.

Tŷ Newydd has continued to grow and develop since those first years. Gillian was the first Chairman of Tŷ Newydd. What hours we spent in those dreaded first Board meetings, endlessly discussing (in English, Welsh and paraphrase) our constitution, our aims and objectives, our lack of finance and thus imminent demise (thwarted, of course), the choice of curtains in the library, marketing and fundraising, and the sign at the bottom of the road. But these were the meetings which laid the foundations, which clarified our ideals and which gave us the vision. Board meetings today are simultaneously translated and mercifully shorter. The ethos, aims and objectives of Tŷ Newydd were established in those long ago meetings and so although we still discuss our lack of finance and thus imminent demise and the sign at the bottom of the road, which still isn't there, we are sure about what we are and that we have a role to play in the literary world of Wales.

Tŷ Newydd is currently in its seventh year. The programme

of courses for adults grows in breadth as well as length every year, attempting to stimulate and consolidate and provide for as many tastes and levels of expertise as possible. We have combined writing with painting, printing, music and mask-making, we've centred courses round such diverse subjects as myth, gay identity and trees—and storytelling is now an integral part of the programme. There is the traditional and the experimental, opportunities for experienced writers but courses, too, which aim to nurture young writers.

And Gillian remains a staunch supporter, an ambassador and, from time to time, a course tutor. The Taliesin Trust and all writers who benefit from their stay at Tŷ Newydd owe her a great deal.

Sally Baker

Sally Baker

74

Waking up the Words

There is a richness about contact with Gillian Clarke that nurtures imaginative life and provides a context for writing. It is partly to do with her extraordinary energy ('this week, Swansea and Yorkshire, then Clwyd, and Aldeborough'), her knowledge of and enthusiasm for literature, but most of all I think in the love of words she communicates.

> Ga puts Mentholatum on her sciatica
> and Ceri soaks the clothes in Parozone

must be her first poem, chanted as she stamped about in her three-year-old world or, crouched in the secret cave under the table of gossiping adults, tapped out the rhythm of sentences and sounded out mysterious overheard words to herself. I seem to recall that repeated syllable-savouring of 'diarrhoea' got her into trouble one polite tea-time. I know about the 'friends' and 'wonderful strangers' that she made tunes out of and about more recent favourites like 'perihelion' and 'pandemonium' because she tells children about them and I am lucky enough to have been there.

My head is full of things Gillian has said—about hiding ideas inside things; how 'Having a good word in your head is like keeping a smooth stone in your pocket, to keep warm and silky with stroking. Words like to be stroked.' I remember that the smell of bonfires reminds her of the brown coat with the velvet collar that she wore, with a woolly bonnet and mittens, when she rode through the streets on her uncle's cart, jumping down to pick up spent fireworks whenever he stopped to deliver milk from the churn. I have shared her excitement at finding the print of magpie's wings in the snow; the stillness of the night broken by the hare's scream she heard with Frances Horowitz; the shock of the ladder slipping under her and of the heron that almost crashed into her windscreen flying across the motorway. Someone once said to me 'Gillian sees amazing things,' and I think it is true.

Why these details are remembered, when so much else evaporates, must be down to the power of the telling. The flavour of talk with her is stored in memory: walking through the woods near Tan-y-Bwlch or with long vistas of the sea but more often among rows of desks, chalk and school disinfectant smells. She was the first writer I met off the page and the first I heard speaking directly to me. My first encounter with her work was a revelation. Standing on a chair clearing a top shelf in the classroom I'd gone back to after some years' busy childcare and rural living (which perhaps explains my ignorance) I came across a photocopied poem.

> I am sitting in a strange room listening
> For the wrong baby

I read, drawn in at once by personal narrative and the simplicity of the statement. My first book was just about to be published and I was feeling lucky and triumphant; one of my aims was to write plainly, even at the risk of being prosaic. 'I don't love/This baby . . .' My first reaction was a leap of recognition—this was a world I knew made real in words; then a hot wave of jealousy. This was real writing, this certainty of phrasing and confidence that the details of working, domestic life could be made into poetry. I wanted to have written it. There was no name: whose work *was* this? I hadn't learned that Gillian had visited the school as a Writer on Tour. The three imperfectly-typed stanzas were more disturbing and immediate than anything I'd found in a book. I read them over and over, while the cooling-down school creaked around me in its long after-four sigh of relief and the clatter of cleaners' buckets drew closer.

Within a year I'd met her and seen her in action. First tutoring a Creative Writing course at Llysfasi, run by the Welsh Academy, then regularly at the Gwynedd A Level

Writing Weekends and working in various schools, later at Tŷ Newydd, always transmitting, apparently casually, in conversation, so much background information about poets and their ideas that it created a context for writing and must often have alerted students or children to a name or a title to look out for. Quoting Robert Frost, 'a fresh look and a fresh listen', referring to Holub, Douglas Dunn, David Jones, Coleridge, George Macbeth, the Mabinogion, Yeats and a hundred others. 'Oh, *yes*, Annie Dillard!' with the infectious enthusiasm of a born teacher. Though she always insists she has never been one, she is a teacher in the best sense of 'educating', leading out ideas in what amounts to philosophical enquiry, of asking and answering questions to oneself. 'Do we think in words?' she once asked a group of eleven year-olds and later I watched her successfully challenge five year-olds to create a planet's ecosystem and then create names and voices for its most significant features. The moon introduced itself as Darklighter; the rainbow's name was Haleliwia. I saw older pupils excited about radio waves, and microscopes: 'Scientists can see inside every cell in your body!', the inner life of dreams, the beginnings of the Solar System, dolphins in Cardigan Bay; moved by accounts of young boys in coalmines, a fossil icthyosaur, a grandmother's shawl. She brings legend to life: poems in *I Can Move the Sea* testify to the force of her re-tellings of Blodeuwedd and the Lady of Llyn-Y-Fan Fach. It is a sort of vision of the wholeness of existence—of words, too, from ring-games and dipping rhymes, pop songs and advertising jingles to Shakespeare and Dylan Thomas.

She has a straightforward technique of getting children going—a series of questions or guided writing exercises that build confidence—'Follow me this time so you can make your own way next.' A nine-year-old suggests the geode he holds is like a doorknob. You see the idea flare in her eyes, and she prompts imagination forward: 'Yes—a doorknob to where? If you could use it to open a door, what might you find?'

Her ideas might not all be new but, borrowed or original, she transmits them in a way that works, both practical and inspirational, and that teachers can pick up so that they might become facilitators of this activity that enhances the sense of self, sharpening memory and awareness. 'Be 100% alive,' she instructs, handing round objects from her bag of tricks—shell or ammonite, a rainstick, the famous buzzard's skull—'close your eyes so you can listen better, feel, sniff like an animal does.' And 'Wake those words up, shake them up so they don't just say the same old things,' introducing games and exercises to help to do it, for instance making alphabetical lists to throw up surprising new connections. 'Leopard light' was one, and 'silence screams/in the space of this skull'; 'eye, hook-hollow, holds/grief.'

'Have a fiddle with it,' she'll say. 'Five minutes!' Then there is invaluable advice about cutting and shaping, not saying too much, how adjectives can blur the focus.

I had taught English for about fifteen years but it took Gillian to show me how to explain simply what a syllable is ('the beat in the word') and to get ten and eleven year-olds chanting the 'ten thumps' of iambic pentameter:

'My name is Nia Roberts, who are you?'

Then they wrote a sonnet! (but without rhyme, 'a terrible trap').

She taught them to read their own words slowly and with authority, to give each word in a poem space to breathe; not to use too many commas, that line-endings are punctuation in a poem; how each of them owns a store of words alive with pictures from their own lives and feelings. How you can make *and break* your own rules, that poetry can be like a ladder, a way out of distress that springs up when it's needed.

What wins children from the first is her lack of standing on ceremony—there is dignity, yes, ritual even—but without the rhetoric and formality teachers maintain. 'I'm not your Miss,

I'm Gillian,' and the class gaze in awe. She talks to four-year-olds with the same enthusiasm and directness—simple but not patronising language—that she will use in a workshop of experienced writers. It's as though she hypnotises them with the quiet confidence of her voice, her responses to each contribution quickening their imaginations so that she can draw original images out even from the surly year 9 boy or a giggle of pert girls. Despite buses leaving or break-time urgencies, there are always groups hanging back to ask or offer something of their own lives. And she would send their work back, transformed from blotched scrawl or straggly jottings into a typed, spaced poem. That investment of interest and time gave a dramatic boost to the confidence of writing in school and must have influenced a whole generation of pupils and teachers. Like other schools, we tried other writers: all were interesting, some inspiring. But none of them were Gillian.

Studying her poetry as part of a literary course prompts a similar response from students as it did from me. Accessible at many different levels, from year 8 to 13, the richness of detail and abundant imagery stimulates them to write their own. 'Letter from a Far Country' is especially valuable for this, and even in 1997 by no means *passé*. The sense of fertility and of the way our lives are part of the mysterious force of nature, the pattern and music of it, have stimulated many lyrics and several ambitious long poems that are true explorations of family tradition or personal experience.

'All my poems are true stories,' she says, and there's no doubt she is a natural storyteller. The lyrical prose of 'The Blue Man' and 'A Field of Hay', her stories written for Pont, speak to the reader as directly as her poems. Both are strong with sense of place: 'The Blue Man' set by the sea, in a bungalow 'that boomed like a dull drum, thudded, rattled and breathed', 'A Field of Hay' (to be published in *Old Enough*) looking back to the summer countryside of childhood, 'a field that had never been ploughed or seeded but annually renewed itself in successions of orchids, cowslips, buttercups, clover and dog daisies.' A young man, son of his parents' middle age, with sisters who are married strangers, has grown up in a chapel house between graveyard and the hayfield that is the limit of his world, only half-aware of the danger of buried memories, of a quarrel between his father and the neighbour Elwyn Price: 'The birds and the child moved unharmed through fortifications of bush and briar, over a mined hayfield.' The story develops a mythical quality of conflict surviving into old age, even to the brink of death, like Laurie Lee's comic Grannies, but carries the germ of tragedy twenty-one years to its resolution—recognition, and a healing continuity: 'Dafydd's off home with Sue for the summer, to rev the engine in the lane, to drive his sick father on little outings to the sea, and to cut the hay in the old field.'

The last word of 'The Blue Man', in which the first-person narrator recalls her thirteenth year with a mixture of delight and sadness and guilt, is 'forgiven'. There are so many strands in this story, it invites the reader in so openly to find personal meaning, that it seems limiting to say what it's 'about'. It is full of a sense of loss, of not wanting things to change but realising they must: 'I don't want gardens to get all brambly, houses to have broken windows or people to die.' And the girl charts her own metamorphosis, from lonely child 'after the split' between her parents, uneasily held between cultures ('My mother kept her meanest voice for Welsh, probably because of her and Dad not getting on') fearful of ghosts and spiders in the summerhouse to confident undergraduate (English, Welsh and Archaeology). The year of the story is the turning point, three elderly sisters who had travelled the world collecting treasures are catalysts. These characters are realised through affectionate details of appearance, habits and possessions. 'Elder Miss Finch had collected the books, younger Miss Finch the rugs and butterflies.' The third sister, 'untidier and jollier' has white curls, a dead archaeologist husband and his money in Bolivia, a cabinet of flints and ammonites, shards of pottery—and a three-thousand-year-old Egyptian grave god figurine which becomes the girl's thirteenth birthday gift. The story explores relationships and the complexities of growing up at a deeper level than other 'worthy' writing for young people; when asked to offer an alternative title, no teenage reader has suggested 'The Birthday Present'. Like the girl, they realise the value of the object is not what makes it special, not even the almost magic way the blue glass face seems to smile as it's turned. ('Once someone has smiled at you, you can't forget it. The face has chosen you.') There is sadness, awareness of inevitable loss ('Like everyone else, they would go') even at the moment of celebration and the final paragraph begins:

> In my head is a derelict house full of the sea wind, and round it the world is falling to ruin . . .

But she still has the Blue Man, the link with the sisters and their world in which she remade herself like one of the brilliant butterflies transforming inside its chrysalis.

With the economy of a well-made poem, the story reminds us of feelings from earlier lives: the awkwardness of not wanting to choose what is most desired; the puzzle of parental disapproval; keeping new passions from friends lest they be spoiled (in this case, The Moonlight Sonata); simple delight in food ('bits of leek and carrot and turnip bobbing in the bowl and home-made rolls freckled like the old ladies' hands') and *things* again: 'a book of Welsh poetry bound in green leather . . . hand-printed on hand-made paper with rough edges and on every sheet you could see a pale pattern like a little sickle when you held it against the light. The initials were printed in dark red, but best of all were the pictures: engravings of waterfalls, woods, whirlpools and lovers. They made me ache.' That's the grace of accuracy, solidity of specification, love.

The sense of being a child is evoked in *A Field of Hay* in a very different way. Learning verses to recite in chapel, Dafydd feels 'a lump under his heart like a heavy dinner.' But the story is just as rewarding, leaving space for the reader to explore. The prose in both bears the hallmarks of Gillian's style—concern for exact phrasing, sensory detail, focussed image, rhythm carrying the charge of feeling. 'Lapis lazuli!'

'It had begun long before Dafydd was born.' Rich, well-crafted sentences are leaping out at me from these two short pieces. 'Occasionally came a glory of some kind—the year of the dandelion, for example, when the field sang sharp gold before the seed-clocks flew in swarms and it was time to cut it down.' There is a wealth of implied meaning (for classroom finding!): 'The invisible sun, camera and photographer looked into the face of the dazzled boy in the picture and were reflected there.'

There's an echo there of 'Siege', and both stories share a characteristic concern with the past, loss and healing, identity and belonging, and other themes that echo Gillian's poetry. Although written for a young audience, they are no less of an achievement and Welsh writing in English is the richer for having them.

In none of Gillian Clarke's work is there is any sense of what other poets have referred to as a struggle with language, wrestling with words, only an abiding and self-perpetuating passion. She is fierce in their defence. When, fearful of the charge of self-conscious 'Welshery', I suggested a few changes to 'The Blue Man', she came back strongly: '*Bara brith* is not fruit cake. Everyone knows what it is. They sell it in Tesco!' quoting Hopkins, Heaney and Hughes on the vigour of real things in real language.

I read somewhere once that poets should seem to be more alive, more lyrical, more optimistic than the rest of us. That fits Gillian. In the end, it is a wholehearted commitment to the moment that makes her work—teaching and writing—special, her capacity to marvel at and enjoy the trash and wonder of the world; to celebrate the variety, as she mused once at the end of a session with sixth-formers, 'disco *and* symphony, strobelights *and* sunsets.'

And, at least in Wales, her influence is everywhere, her tracks easy to follow. Yesterday, for instance. Gwynedd A Level English teachers met to moderate coursework at Plas Glynllifon, in a room with several large wall-hangings of textile representations of Blodeuwedd. There has been a primary-school teacher-training session. On the piano, an owl of paper and card, feather-perfect, crouches with wings just lifting, ready to fly.

Christine Evans

The Writing Room

'If there's one word that sums up everything that's gone wrong since the War, it's Workshop.'

Kingsley Amis, *Jake's Thing*

Imagine a room. A small, College room: cream-wash walls, a green carpet, the chairs and bookcase of polished oak. A bay window with ragged net curtains looked out across the street. It was a cold October evening in 1984. I sat, shivering, in the corner. The shivering was not caused by the ambient temperature of Dewi Hostel, but by sheer terror. This was my first encounter with Gillian Clarke and the newly-formed Lampeter Writers' Workshop. Sue Moules and I were the first to arrive. Luckily, we had known each other at College, because if I was petrified then so, as I later discovered, was Sue. The woman sitting opposite us seemed terrifying. Beautiful, elegant . . . and a Poet. I too wanted to be a Poet, which is why I was there on that dull Tuesday evening. But sitting in the room, with the light softly glowing on the table, and the prospect of actually having to read my work aloud to other people, the only thing I wanted to do was to high-tail it out of there as quickly as possible and disappear into the damp back-streets of Lampeter.

From the start, the room itself became particularly important to us. Though we changed the physical locations of the meetings several times over the years, the room always provided a focal-point, a place where we could write, make friends, exchange ideas. In a small rural community like Lampeter, with a scattered and diverse population, it was the only place where people could get together and concentrate on writing in a focussed way. We drew members from as far away as Brecon, Carmarthen, Aberystwyth, south Wales. For many, we provided the only forum for creative writing in a radius of fifty or sixty miles. We were a mixed bunch:

students, housewives, unemployed, a shepherdess, a film director, academics, ex-Diplomatic service. Somehow, we interacted and got on together; a large part of this is due to Gillian and her democratic leadership of the group.

We shared one building in College with several other groups who also had evening classes. Inevitably, at times there would be mix-ups, wrong rooms allocated, people wandering from door to door uncertain of where they should be. Sometimes, it wasn't until after the coffee-break that we discovered stray French learners, carpenters, farmers and Life-After-Death Part One students, who had wandered into the group by accident and been too embarrassed to admit their mistake. In all probability we also lost a good few poets the same way.

Some evenings closely resembled a scene from a Pinter play. Our room would frequently have been double-booked and there would be the necessary tramp to the Porter's Lodge to fetch the key to another room. Sometimes, this second room would also have someone in it. On the last occasion this occurred, we opened the door to find three men saying their 'Hail Mary's'. Faced with the full weight of the Roman Catholic Church, we expected a rapid back-down from Gillian. But she was in Mexican stand-off mood that evening. Eventually the Hail Mary's lost, and we entered the room triumphant.

In the early years of the workshop, a good few evenings were dominated by what become known as 'Gillian's skull'. It had belonged, we assumed, to a very long-dead sheep, and judging from the expression on its bony face, the death had not been a particularly pleasant one. It was, it has to be said, a fairly gruesome object. Gillian used it mainly as a teaching-aid in schools. The sight of this skull, staring at us across the table did little, I'm afraid, for our poetic imaginations. But she also brought us feathers, pieces of wood shiny with salt and the waves, sea-horses, pictures or coloured stones. We learnt to use these as a basis for our writing. Sometimes there was honey, culled from her own bees, or a wild orchid.

If thirteen years seem a long time for a workshop to continue under the direction of one person, then a glance at the publication record of the group as a whole testifies to the success of what has been achieved. Members of the group have published books of poetry, stories, anthologies, a children's novel, plays and monologues. Others have gained prizes: the Aberystwyth Open, the National, and countless smaller competitions. Others still have taken an active part in poetry readings, courses, the Hay Festival. Three members have won the Writers' Group Prize in the Cardiff International Poetry Competition; three have been awarded Welsh Arts Council bursaries. There is no doubt that the existence and discipline of the workshop continues to encourage and inspire its members, not only because it keeps us writing and talking about our work, but also because of Gillian's firm and continuous leadership.

Gillian has always been both fair and generous; her criticism is only ever constructive. I never remember her losing her temper once, not even on the occasion when a member of the group staggered into the workshop some half-an-hour late and obviously the worse for wear. He slumbered quietly in a chair as the business of the evening progressed. When it came to reading our work around the table, he awoke briefly for his turn, executed a perfect sonnet, and fell back into unconsciousness. Gillian did not turn a hair.

We often made up a group to go and see a visiting writer, or hosted a reading ourselves. One evening we played host to John Tripp; sadly, the last time many of us would see him. The reading unfortunately co-incided with the summer closing of the Students' Union bar, on which occassion the Bar Stewards sold off the remainder of the stock in bulk, and at ludicrously low prices.

Other readings were more sober affairs, and we enjoyed hearing R. S. Thomas, Seamus Heaney, Dannie Abse, Peter Finch and Sheenagh Pugh among others.

It seems improbable that the workshop will last for

another thirteen years. Thanks to the Internet, the interaction of like-minded people is being shifted from small rooms such as ours to a network of communication across the World Wide Web. But perhaps wherever there are writers who value the face-to-face contact with other writers, the good and dedicated leadership of a teacher such as Gillian, and the weekly social and professional debate between people, there will always be those who crave the defined yet intimate atmosphere offered by The Writing Room.

Kathy Miles

Writers' Workshop
for Gillian Clarke

1. Tŷ Newydd

We have come here to write, if we can,
to make shapes of our thoughts and feelings,
perhaps to see what we are part of.

One man remembers magical sensations,
a woman writes about her sister who has died.

Each of us moves restlessly through a maze,
glimpsing older and younger backs or faces,
most of them our own.

Each also senses another presence,
which haunts us in different forms:

the silence of a factory in which the machines
are shrouded in dusty sheets,
the reverberating hush
of a battleground after armistice,
or a man who stamped his image on the world,
and came back here to die,
all his powers, titles, names
                    a memory.

When we gather for a workshop
someone remarks how strange it is
to think of the old man lying here in his last days.

Strange, indeed, when
in the room in which he died
we hear an echo as we stand
at the bay window looking down
over sea and mountains,
as he did, the 'Welsh Wizard'.

2. By Afon Dwyfor

It is an illusion, of course,
but at last the 'Great Commoner'
seems to have become part of the elements—
at one with the boulder built into his memorial,
and Afon Dwyfor swirling between boulders,
and woods of oak and beech and sycamore,
and alders dipping their leaves in the water.

The lichened boulder light shines on
is green and bright orange,
but in my mind it is black—
a memorial to the century
cast in iron.

3. Lloyd George Museum, Llanystumdwy

In one photograph,
a dark-haired poet looks up,
proudly, perhaps defiantly, his arms
laid on the arms of the bardic chair.

He is honoured by principalities and powers,
and perhaps humoured, for the Statesman
who stands beside him, playing his part,
is smiling slightly.
It amazes me to recognise the poet,
who is still young. I saw him in old age:
Gwenallt, the skull showing in his face
which was like parchment where feeling
had etched the history of his people.

The dead, brown leaves
of the laurel wreath are not his.
It was thrown into the carriage
in which the Statesman drove
through London, with the king, returning
in triumph from Versailles.

Surely there are materials here
for a poem about history:
fifty years of cartoons
and newspaper photographs—
manhandled suffragettes
with the clothes clawed off their backs,
munitions, wars, faces in the maze . . .

Or about the man who said
he was prepared 'to thrust even love
itself under the wheels of my juggernaut'.

4. Criccieth: the boy on the beach

We have come here to make order, if we can,
each mazed mind untangling a way; and here
for a time we create harmony among ourselves,
each one sensing what the other sees.

Below the house, field paths lead us,
out of the dusty empire of the sun,
to a smell of wild roses and brine,
peeling, upturned boats, crab-shells
and fleshy, salt-loving plants.

Here it is always another world.
Two crows, out of an old ballad,
pick over kelp at the water's edge,
hop back when a wave breaks.

He would have been amused, the boy
who played on this pebbly beach,
below the castle,
and perhaps the old man, too,
standing here again,
as the great idea that had driven him
faded, with his offices and titles.
Small again,
with everything still to make,
his companions would be once more the powers that shape rock,
and make and unmake cloud,
which drifts over on a day that he feels will last for ever,
darkening, brightening.

Jeremy Hooker

Gweithdy

'Mae hi'n debyg i gragen
'—i blisgyn ŵy
'—i belen ping-pong
'—i gwpan blastig mas o beiriant coffi
'—i lythyr gan gefnder y'ch chi heb ei weld ers meitin'

dyma ni, grynwyr, yn estyn llond dwrn o anadl
o law i law. Tu ôl i'n llygaid cau,
mae'r meddwl sy' rhyngom ni yn fawr fel rhewlif,
a'n bysedd yn sgrialu i gydio, rhywsut,
yn hanfod y dieithrwch hwn
cyn troi, a'i dywallt i gawg y dwylo nesa'—

minnau fel blaidd yn sbio rhwng fy mysedd
i weld wynebau'r plant, eu llygaid stwn,
a'r syniad hwn sy'n symud trwy'r distawrwydd
fel adain fawr sy'n curo môr o olau,

a gweld
eu bod nhw'n deall, nawr,
mai penglog boda yw'r rhisgl hwn sy'n debyg
i fyrdd o bethau, yn dywyll ac yn olau
—cragen y falwen wedi pig y fronfraith
y pant mewn cae sy'n dal y rhew a'i gadw;
dyrnaid o dywyllwch sy'n disgwyl cannwyll;
anrheg fechan mae arnaf ofn ei hagor
amlen o asgwrn heb stamp, heb un cyfeiriad

Elin ap Hywel

Workshop

'It's like an eggshell
'—a shuttlecock
'—a seashell
'—a paper cup on a street corner
'—an airmail letter from an unknown country—'

we shunt this breath of a thing
quakerish, from hand to hand, eyes closed,
our concentration cupped between us,
fingers slaloming to touch
something about it before we pass it on—

I cheat, open my eyes and see
the children's faces sucked in tight
by this idea which is moving through the silence,
a rush of feathers beating fields of light—

and now they know

that this blown egg is a bird's skull,
and so is other things too:
a snail shell after the thrush's beak;
the hollow in the hill that's full of frost;
a handful of dark that's waiting for a match;
A tiny box you'd be afraid to open.
An envelope of bone without a stamp.

Elin ap Hywel

Looking into the Field

From the five corners of the field
they lift their heads and move towards him.
This is the man who brings food.
His collie presses against the window
of the Land Rover and leaves a nose-round watermark.
He walks to the four still legs of a dead sheep
and bends to grasp fistfuls of tight wool.
Lifting from his knees he pulls and rolls
the ewe upright, setting the legs kicking again.
Tubful of life, she bleats and waddles to new grass.
The field has been put to rights and as he walks back
his flock return to their grass and the first autumn leaves.
Four disappointed crows flap into the sky she'd
stared up through like a cloudy blue tunnel.

Tony Curtis

Images

(An attempt to convey the atmosphere of poems from *Letter from a Far Country* studied for coursework)

Gillian Clarke

She is afternoon, late summer
gathering in washing strung between
old fruit trees, humming as she remembers
her grandmother's white lace, her recipe
for bread and the welcoming warmth
of her flowered apron. She is ripening
like corn and summer plums and children.
She is a leaping seal, a white mare dreaming
as the full moon rises.

Poetry Book

Thoughts are stored whole
in this book, rich as cream
in a jug under a beaded net
on a slate pantry shelf, cool
though outside's hot and itchy
with haymaking.

Each poem has its own taste
like a drink of spring water
from a bottle bright as a blue iris
or from a clear, deep well
where sometimes you can see yourself.

Group poems by Year 12 pupils at Ysgol Glan-y-Môr, Pwllheli 1992-3

Selective Bibliography: Gillian Clarke

Section One: Work by Gillian Clarke

POETRY COLLECTIONS

Clarke, Gillian. *Snow on the Mountain*. Christopher Davies, 1971.
Clarke, Gillian. *The Sundial*. Gomer, 1978.
Clarke, Gillian. *Letter From A Far Country*. Manchester: Carcanet, 1982.
Clarke, Gillian. *Selected Poems*. Manchester: Carcanet, 1985.
Clarke, Gillian. *Letting in the Rumour*. Manchester: Carcanet, 1989.
Clarke, Gillian. *Harvest at Mynachlog*. Gwasg Gregynog, 1990.
Clarke, Gillian. *The King of Britain's Daughter*. Manchester: Carcanet, 1993.

INDIVIDUAL POEMS
Anglo-Welsh Review:
> 19.44 'Journey'
> 'Death of a Young Woman'
> 'Baby Sitting'
> 20.46 'Community'
> 'Two Working'
> 'Tom Cat' (uncollected)
> 22.50 'Watching Storms' (uncollected)
> 'Return to Penarth'

New England Review and Bread Loaf Quarterly:
> 10/4 'At One Thousand Feet' (1988)
> 'Neighbours'

New Welsh Review:
> 1 'Listening for Trains', p 81.
> 7 'At St Winefride's Well', p 24. ('St Winefride's Well' in *KBD*)
> 13 'On Air'

Planet :
> 35 'Last Rites'
> 74 'Cofiant'

PNR:
> 29 'A Journal from France'
> 36 'Journey'
> 'Dyddgu replies to Dafydd'
> 'Waterfall'
> 'East Moors'

97

'Sunday'
'Scything'
22.3   'Cold Knap Lake'
'Tory Party Conference, Bournemouth, 1986'
'Oranges'
32.2   'Women's Work' (uncollected)
'Balancing' (uncollected)

COMPILATIONS IN WHICH INCLUDED:
Anglo-Welsh Poetry 1480-1980. Ed. Garlick & Mathias. Poetry Wales Press, 1984.
    'Blaen Cwrt'   'Hay-making'
    'Lunchtime Lecture'   'Ram'
    'Foghorns'   'Suicide on Pentwyn Bridge'

Between the Severn and the Wye: Poems of the Border Counties of England and Wales. Selected by Johnny Coppin. The Windrush Press.

The Bright Field. Ed. Meic Stephens. Carcanet, 1991.
    'The Hare'   from 'Cofiant'
   . 'Llŷr' from   'Letter from a Far Country'
    'Neighbours'   'Overheard in County Sligo'
    'Seal'

A Cardiff Anthology. Ed. Meic Stephens. Bridgend: Seren, 1987.
    'Suicide on Pentwyn Bridge'
    'East Moors'
    'Cardiff Elms'
plus: 'Missa Pontcanna' in second edition.1996.

Common Ground. Ed. Susan Butler. Cardiff: Poetry Wales Press, 1985.
    'Letter to a Far Country'   'Buzzard'
    'The Water Diviner'   'East Moors'

Dragon's Hoard. Ed. Sam Adams & Gwilym Rees Hughes. Llandysul: Gomer, 1976.
    'Guinea Pigs'

Exchanges: Poems by Women In Wales. Ed. Jude Brigley. Dinas Powys: Honno Press, 1990.
    'Miracle on St David's Day' p 5.
    'Swinging' p 10.
    'Lunchtime Lecture' p 22.
    'Neighbours' p 50.
    'Heron at Port Talbot' p 63.
    'Last Rites' p 74.
    'Missa Pontcanna' p 85.

The Faber Book of 20th Century Women's Poetry. Ed. Fleur Adcock. London: Faber and Faber, 1987.
'Babysitting'

The Forward Book of Poetry. London: Forward Press, 1994.
'Anorexic'

Green Horse. Ed. Meic Stephens and Peter Finch. Swansea: C. Davies, 1978.
'Blaen Cwrt'   'The Sundial'
'Sailing'   'Dyddgu replies to Dafydd'
'Harvest at Mynachlog'   'Beechbuds'
'Birth'   'Lunchtime Lecture'

The Kilpeck Anthology. Ed. Glenn Storhaug. Five Seasons Press, 1981.
'She' ('Sheila na Gig at Kilpeck')

The Mountains of Wales. Ed. Ioan Bowen Rees. Cardiff: University of Wales Press, 1992.
'Snow on the Mountain'   'At One Thousand Feet'

Poems '71. Ed. Jeremy Hooker. Llandysul: Gomer, 1971.
'Still Life' 'The Sundial'   'Nightride' 'Catrin'

Poems '72. Ed. John Ackerman. Llandysul: Gomer, 1972.
'Storm Awst'   'Tom Cat'
'Solo'

Poems '73. Ed. Gwyn Ravage, Llandysul: Gomer, 1973.
'Dyddgu replies to Dafydd' 'Lunchtime Lecture'
'In Pisgah Graveyard'

Poems '74. Ed. Peter Elfed Lewis. Llandysul: Gomer, 1974.
'Burning Nettles'   'Swinging'
'Sheep's Skulls'

Poems '76. Ed. Glyn Jones. Llandysul: Gomer, 1976.
'St Thomas's Day'   'Choughs'

Poems '78. Ed. Graham Allen. Llandysul: Gomer, 1978.
'Last Rites'   'The Ram'

Poesie Des Regions D'Europe: Poèmes du Pays de Galles. Sélection et introduction Tony Curtis, Traduction française, Christine Pagnoulle. Namur: Revue de la Maison de la Poesie, 1994.
'The Hare'/*'Le lièvre'*   'The Ram'/*'Le bélier'*
'Choughs'/*'Les craves'*

Poetry Book Society Anthology 1986/7. Ed. Jonathan Barker.
'Windmill'

Poetry Book Society Anthology 1988/9. Ed. David Constantine.
'Neighbours'   'Mother'

Poetry Book Society Anthology 1. Ed. Fraser Steel.
'Swimming with Seals'

Poetry Book Society Anthology 3. Ed. Anne Stevenson.
'Hölderlin'

Poetry Book Society Bulletin. Summer 1993 no 157.
'Olwen takes her first steps on the word processor in time of war'.

The Poetry of Pembrokeshire. Ed. Tony Curtis. Bridgend: Seren, 1989.
'Wild Orchids'   'Gannet'.
'Seal'

The Poetry of Snowdonia. Ed. Tony Curtis. Bridgend: Seren, 1989.
'Climbing Cader Idris'.   'Clywedog'
'Castell y Bere'   'Fires on Llŷn'
'Sailing'

Poetry Wales 25 Years. Ed. Cary Archard. Seren, 1990.
'Plums' p 164.

Six Women Poets. Ed. Judith Kinsman. Oxford: Oxford University Press, 1992.
'Letter from a Far Country'   'Siege'
'Miracle on St David's Day'   'Overheard in County Sligo'
'Login'   'East Moors'
'The Sundial'   'Last Rites'
'Scything'   'Still Life'
'Marged'   'White Roses'

Sixty Women Poets. Ed. Linda France. Bloodaxe, 1993.
'The Water Diviner'   'On Air'
'Overheard in County Sligo'   'Breakers Yard'
'Red Poppy'

Ten Anglo-Welsh Poets. Ed. Sam Adams. Cheadle: Carcanet, 1974.
'Death of a Young Woman'   'Still Life'
'Journey'   'Birth'
'Dyddgu Replies to Dafydd'   'The Sundial'
'Lunchtime Lecture'   'Blaen Cwrt'
'Lines'   'Burning Nettles'
'Waterfall'

The Third Day: Landscapes and the Word: An Anthology of Poems and Photographs. Ed. Kathy Miles. Llandysul: Gomer, 1995.
    'Hafod' (uncollected).

The Urgency of Identity: Contemporary English-language poetry from Wales. Ed. David Lloyd. Evanston, Illinois: Triquarterly Books, Northwestern University Press, 1994.

'Plums'	'Sheila na Gig at Kilpeck'
'Fires on Llŷn'	'Llŷr'
'Windmill'	'Seal'
'Neighbours'	'Blodeuwedd'.

The Virago Book of Birth Poetry. Ed. Charlotte Otten. London: Virago, 1993.
    'Sheila na Gig at Kilpeck'   'Scything'

Twentieth Century Anglo-Welsh Poetry. Ed. Dannie Abse. Seren. (forthcoming).

Wales: An Anthology. Ed. Alice Thomas Ellis. London: Collins, 1989.
    'Climbing Cader Idris.'

BOOKS, NOT POETRY COMPILATIONS, IN WHICH INCLUDED:

The Page's Drift: R.S. Thomas at Eighty. Ed. M. Wynn Thomas. Seren: 1993.
    'The Poet'

Thirteen Ways of Looking at Tony Conran. Ed. Nigel Jenkins. Llanishen: The Welsh Union of Writers, 1995.
    'Green Man' (Uncollected).

TRANSLATIONS
Cell Angel. (by Menna Elfyn). Newcastle: Bloodaxe, 1996. (Some of the poems are translated by Gillian Clarke.)
    (Translator's Comments. p 8.)
    'Snowman' p 13.
    'Double Bed' p 15.
    'Sweet Grapes' p 19
    'Cell Angel' p 21/3.
    'Psalm to the Little Gap in the Cell Door' p 25.
    'Next Door' p 29.
    'Nunnery' p 31.
    'No 257863 H.M.P.' p 33.
    'Pomegranates' p 51.
    'Amber (for Tony Conran)' p 53.
    'Hairdresser' p 67/9.
    'Pigeons in Ebbw Vale' p 79.

101

Eucalyptus: Selected Poems 1978-94. (by Menna Elfyn) Gomer, 1995.
'The year of the bat, 1986' p 3/5
'Phoning home' p 53/55
'Arsenic and gold at Dolaucothi' p 85
'In memory of Kelly' p 103

One Bright Morning. (*Tegwch y Bore* by Kate Roberts.) Unpublished.

One Moonlit Night. (by T. Llew Jones) Llandysul: Pont Books, 1991.

Poetry Review:
83/3 from 'Insomnia' (Marina Tsvetaeva) ('Thirteen Ways of Looking
At Tsvetaeva'.1993)

Poetry Wales:
29.4 'Phoning Home' (Menna Elfyn)

Thirteen Ways of Looking at Tony Conran. Ed. Nigel Jenkins. Llanishen: The
Welsh Union of Writers, 1995:
p 12. 'Amber (for Tony)'. (Menna Elfyn. 'Ambyr (i Tony)').

SHORT STORIES
'The Blue Man'. *The Blue Man & other stories from Wales.* Pont Books, 1994.
'A Field of Hay'. *Old Enough & other stories.* Pont Books, 1997.

PLAYS
Talking to Wordsworth. Radio Play. March 1st, 1997.
The Time of the Wolf. Theatr Powys's autumn/ winter production 1996.

ARTICLES AND INTERVIEWS BY GILLIAN CLARKE:
'Poet on a Bursary.' *Book News From Wales.* Summer, 1981. pp 4-5.

'In Literary Residence.' *Book News From Wales.* Spring, 1985. pp 8-9.

Introduction to own poems.
Butler, Susan. Ed. *Common Ground.* Poetry Wales Press, 1985.
'Hunter-gatherer or madonna mistress?'
Article on women's poetry for *Bloodaxe Catalogue* 1986/7.

'A Mission and a Pleasure'.
PBS Bulletin 133, 1987.

'Beyond the Boundaries: A Symposium on gender in poetry.'
Planet 66, Dec/Jan 1987/8 pp 50-61.

Introduction.
The Poetry Book Society Anthology 1987/8. London: Hutchinson, 1987.

'*Letting in the Rumour:* A Letter from a Far Country by Gillian Clarke'.
PBS Bulletin 141, 1989.

'The Making of Child-Poets.' *Book News From Wales.* Winter 1989. pp 5-6.

Introduction to own poems, reasons for selection.
The Bright Field. Ed. Meic Stephens, 1991.

Introduction to own poems.
Six Women Poets. Oxford: Oxford University Press, 1992.

'Voice of the Tribe.' *Regionalität, Nationalität und Internationalität in der zeitgenossischen Lyrik.* University of Tübingen, 1992.

'Writer's Diary'. *Books In Wales.* Spring, 1993. p 4.

'Tall Tales Remade'.
PBS Bulletin. Summer 1993, no 157.

'Beginning with Bendigeidfran'.
Our Sisters' Land. Eds. Jane Aaron, Teresa Rees, Sandra Betts, Moira Vincentelli, Cardiff, UWP, 1994.

'Interview'.
The Urgency of Identity: Contemporary English-language poetry from Wales.
Evanston: Illinois: Triquarterly Books, Northwestern University Press, 1994.
pp 25-31.
'Multi-Storey City'. *Times Educational Supplement.* 14.4.1995.

'The King of Britain's Daughter'.
How Poets Work. Ed. Tony Curtis. Bridgend: Seren, 1996. pp 122-136.

EDUCATIONAL WORK
English Literature Anthology: Syllabus B 1998/9. Welsh Joint Education Committee.

    'Stealing Peas'   'Lurcher'
    'The Vet'   'Lament'.
    'Swimming with Seals'

Illustrated Poetry Broadsheets: Writing from Wales. The National Language Unit Brook Street Treforest, Pontypridd.
    1. *People.* 'The Water-diviner.'
    3. *Relationships.* 'My Box.'

Poetry Resources File: for Primary Schools. (BP Education.) London: Poetry Society, 1992.
    'Myth, Life, the Universe and Everything.'
    'A Sense of Place: Singing the World Alive.'

Poetry Resources File: For Secondary Schools. (BP Education.) London: Poetry Society, 1992.
  'Myth, Life, the Universe and Everything.'
  'A Sense of Place: Singing the World Alive.'

Poetry Wales 25.4, 1990.
  'Re-making the World: Poetry in Primary Schools'.

Spoken English. Vol.16 No 3, Sept. 1983. pp 11-13.
  'Paragraphs of arrows: sharing the experience of poetry in schools.'

Wall to Wall Poetry.
  'Hay-Making'.

REVIEWS BY GILLIAN CLARKE

1. *Eryri, The Mountains of Longing* by Amory Lovins. *Authors of Wales Today*. Ed. Geoffrey Hardley-Tayson. *Anglo-Welsh Review* 49, 1973. pp 287-8, p 299.

2. *Murder at the Eisteddfod* by J. Ellis Williams and *Lady with a Cool Eye* by Gwen Moffatt. *Anglo-Welsh Review* 51, 1974. pp 168-70.

3. *Conundrum* by Jan Morris. *Anglo-Welsh Review* 53, 1974. p 259.

4. *Mountains, Polecats, Pheasants and Other Elegies* by Leslie Norris. *Poetry Wales* 9.4. 1974,   p 95.

5. *The Human Face* by John Liggett. *Anglo-Welsh Review* 54, 1975. pp 268-8.

6. *I Sent a Letter to My Wife* by Bernice Rubens. *Anglo-Welsh Review* 56, 1976. pp 206-8.

7. *Cornish Short Stories* Ed. by Denys Val Baker. Penguin. *Anglo-Welsh Review* 57, 1976. pp 201-4.

8. *Rebel's Progress* by T. Farley. *Powys Review.* 1981, Vol 2. pp 87-8.

9. *Between Here and Now* by R.S.Thomas. *Anglo-Welsh Review* 71, 1982. pp 80-83.

10. *Burning Brambles.* by Roland Matthias. *Book News from Wales*. Aut. 1983 p 10.

11. *Selected Poems* by Fleur Adcock. *Powys Review* 17, 1985.

12. *Selected Poems 1970-1985* by Tony Curtis and *Falling Back* by Christine Evans. *Book News From Wales*. Sum.1987, p 12.

13. *Poems: 1965-75* by Margaret Atwood. Virago. *Poetry Wales* 27.1, 1991.

14. *The Oslo Tram* by Oliver Reynolds; *Flight Patterns* by John Davies; *Selected Poems* by Derek Mahon. *New Welsh Review* 14, 1991, pp 74-76.

15. 'Belonging to the same world.' *Unconditional Surrender* by Emyr Humphreys. *Planet* 121. 1997. pp 95-6.

16. 'Heart of the matter: Gillian Clarke reads an Auden to Zephaniah of love poetry'. *The Kingfisher Book of Poems about Love* chosen by Roger McGough; *A Spell of Words* by Elizabeth Jennings; *We Couldn't Provide Fish Thumbs*. *Times Educational Supplement 2*. 14.2.1997. p 7.

17. Other books reviewed recently in the *Times Educational Supplement* include: *Griffin's Castle* by Jenny Nimmo; *Plex* by Philip Grosse; *The Magic Apostrophe* by Jenny Sullivan; *Sophie's Ghost* by Catherine Johnson; *Something's Burning* by Mary Oldham; *Talking Turkeys* by Benjamin Zephania; *Great Snakes* by Kit Wright; *The Utter Nutters* by Brian Patten; *Plenty of Time* by Brian Morse; *Three has Gone* by Jackie Kay; *Grandfather's Old Bruk-a-down Car* by John Egard; *The Weather Getting Verse* by Andrew Peters; *Cock Crow to Starlight,* chosen by Rumer Godden; *Teaching the Parrot* by Richard Edwards; *Growing Up in Wales 1895-1939* by Jeffrey Grenfell-Hill.

EDITORIAL WORK:
Anglo-Welsh Review:

50, 1973.	Roland Mathias and Gillian Clarke.
51, 1974.	Roland Mathias and Gillian Clarke.
52, 1974	Roland Mahias and Gillian Clarke.
53, 1974.	Roland Mathias and Gillian Clarke.
54, 1975.	Roland Mathias and Gillian Clarke.
55, 1975/6.	Roland Mathias and Gillian Clarke.
56, 1976.	Roland Mathias and Gillian Clarke.
57, 1976.	Gillian Clarke and John Davies
58, 1977.	Gillian Clarke and John Davies.
59, 1977.	Gillian Clarke and John Davies.
60, 1978	Gillian Clarke and John Davies. G.C. Editorial.
61, 1978.	Gillian Clarke and John Davies.
62, 1978	Gillian Clarke and John Davies.
63, 1979.	Gillian Clarke and John Davies.
64, 1979.	Gillian Clarke and John Davies.
65, 1979	Gillian Clarke and Tony Bianchi.
66, 1980.	Gillian Clarke and Tony Bianchi.
67, 1980.	Gillian Clarke and Tony Bianchi.
68, 1981	Gillian Clarke and Greg Hill.
69, 1981.	Gillian Clarke and Greg Hill. G.C. Editorial.
71, 1982.	Gillian Clarke and Greg Hill. G.H. Editorial.
72, 1982.	Gillian Clarke and Greg Hill. G.C. Editorial.
73, 1983.	Gillian Clarke and Greg Hill. G.H. Editiorial.
74, 1983.	Gillian Clarke and Greg Hill. G.C. Editorial.
75, 1984.	Gillian Clarke and Greg Hill. G.H. Editorial.
76, 1984.	Gillian Clarke and Greg Hill. G.C. Editorial.
77, 1984.	Gillian Clarke and Greg Hill. G.H. Editorial.
78, 1985	Roland Mathias thanking Gillian Clarke.

I Can Move the Sea: 100 Poems by Children.(Chosen by Gillian Clarke.) Llandysul: Pont Books, 1996.

The Whispering Room: A Collection of Haunted Poems. Kingfisher Books, 1996.

Section 2: Other Writers On Gillian Clarke

REVIEWS OF GILLIAN CLARKE'S POETRY

Snow on the Mountain
1. Randal Jenkins. *Anglo-Welsh Review* 47, 1972.
2. David Shayer. *Poetry Wales* 8.1, 1972, pp 70-72.
3. John Barnie. 'Diesels and Sundials'. *Planet* 49/50, Jan 1980.

The Sundial
1. Gerald Morgan. *Anglo-Welsh Review* 63, 1978.
2. Gerard Werson. *Poetry Wales* 14.3, 1978/9, pp 82-5.
3. Priscilla Eckhard. 'Directness and Indirection'. *Poetry Review* 69.1, 1979.
4. Anon. *Book News From Wales*. Autumn 1978. p 31.
5. Jeremy Hooker. 'Inside Knowledge.' *PNR* 29, 1982.

Letter from a Far Country
1. Philip Owens. Anglo-*Welsh Review* 75, 1984.
2. Robert Nisbet. 'Poems in Radio'. *Anglo-Welsh Review* 65, 1976.
3. Michael O'Neill. 'Urbanity Disturbed'. *Poetry Review* 3.2, 1983 pp 58-60.

Selected Poems
1. Pamela Stewart. 'Winning Ground'. *Planet* 52, 1985.
2. Jo Lloyd. *Poetry Wales* 21/1, 1985, pp 121-5.
3. Anne Stevenson. *Powys Review* 17, 1985.
4. Martin Hazlehurst. *Anglo-Welsh Review* 81, 1985.
5. Denis Donoghue. 'Ten Poets'. *London Review of Books*. 7.11.1985.
6. Tony Curtis. 'Common Ground'. *Poetry Review* 75.4, 1985 pp 62-65.
7. Greg Hill. *Book News From Wales*. Autumn, 1985. p 9.

Letting in the Rumour
1. Cynthia Fuller. *New Welsh Review*. 7, 1989, p 82.
2. Simon Ponsford. *Poetry Wales* 25.3. 1989.
3. Mark Wormald. 'Tracking her Sources'. *Times Literary Supplement*. 5.10.1989, p 1065.
4. Mercer Simpson. *Powys Review* 25, 1990.
5. Pamela Stewart.'An Expanding World'.*Planet* 77, Nov 1989, pp 94-6.
6. Sheenagh Pugh. 'Peak Viewing'. *Poetry Review* 80.1, 1990.

The King of Britain's Daughter
1. Belinda Humfrey. *Poetry Wales* 29.2, 1993.
2. Tony Conran. *New Welsh Review* 23, 1993.
3. Catherine Fisher.'The Past and its People'.*Planet* 104, 1994, pp 95-6.
4. Roger Garfitt. 'Elevenses'. *Poetry Review* 84.2, 1994.
5. Des Clifford. *Books In Wales*. Autumn 1993. p 15.

REVIEWS OF COMPILATIONS

Between the Severn and the Wye: Poems of the Border Counties of England and Wales.
1. Anne Cluysenaar. 'Not Fixed but Sliding'. *Planet 106*, Aug/Sept. 1994. pp 100-102.

The Bright Field
1. Jeremy Hooker. 'Questions of Identity'. *Planet* 87, June/July 1991, pp 59-65.
2. Edwin Morgan. *Poetry Wales* 27.4, 1992.
3. Dannie Abse. 'Talking not Singing.' *New Welsh Review.* 13.1991. pp 41-42.
4. Greg Hill. *Book News From Wales.* Aut. 1993. p 9/10.

Common Ground
1. Philip Pacey. *Poetry Wales* 1985.
2. Gerald Morgan. *Anglo-Welsh Review* 81, 1985. pp 108-11.
3. M. Wynn Thomas. *Book News From Wales.* Winter 1985. p 8.

Eucalyptus: Selected Poems 1978-94. (by Menna Elfyn)
1. Catherine Fisher. 'Affirmations.' *Planet* 114. Dec./Jan. 1995/6. pp 111-113.
2. Dannie Abse. *New Welsh Review* 29. 1995. pp 94-6.
3. Jane Aaron. *Books In Wales.* Aut. 1995. 3/95. p 17/8.
Exchanges: Poems by Women in Wales.
1. Catherine Fisher. 'Out of the Ghetto?' *Planet* 86. 1991.

The Forward Book of Poetry, 1994.
1. John Pikoulis. *New Welsh Review* 25. 1994. pp 72/3.

Poesie Des Regions D'Europe: Poèmes du Pays de Galles.
1. Ceridwen Lloyd-Morgan. 'A Wider Audience.' *Planet* 113, Oct./Nov. 1995, pp 111-113.
2. Mary Parnell. *New Welsh Review* 29, 1995. pp 100-101.
3. Meic Stephens. *Books In Wales.* Sum. 1995 2/95. p 14.

Sixty Women Poets.
1. John Pikoulis. *New Welsh Review* 25. 1994. pp 71-3.
2. Patricia Craig. 'Redressing the Balance.' *Poetry Review* 83/4. Winter 1993/4. pp 59/60.

10 Anglo-Welsh Poets
1. Peter Elfed Lewis. *Anglo-Welsh Review* 24.53, 1974.

The Third Day.
1. Lloyd Rees. *Poetry Wales* 31.4.1996. pp 69-70.

ARTICLES ABOUT GILLIAN CLARKE
Green, Diane. 'Gillian Clarke: Love Poet/ Historian'. *The Swansea Review* 16, 1996. pp 87-92.

Hooker, Jeremy. "A Big Sea Running in a Shell': the Poetry of Gillian Clarke'.*The Presence of the Past*. Bridgend: Poetry Wales Press, 1987. (in *Anglo-Welsh Review* and in *PNR* 50)
Peach, Linden. 'Incoming Tides'. *New Welsh Review* 1, 1989.

Peach, Linden. 'Igniting Pent Silences'. *Ancestral Lines: Culture and Identity in the Work of Six Contemporary Poets*. Seren, 1992.

Smith, K.E. 'The Poetry of Gillian Clarke'. *Poetry in the British Isles: Non-Metropolitan Perspectives*. Eds. Hans-Werner Ludwig and Lothat Fietz. Cardiff: University of Wales Press, 1995. pp 267-281.

Thomas, M.Wynn. 'Place, Race and Gender in the poetry of Gillian Clarke'. *Essays in Memory of Tudor Bevan*. Cardiff: University of Wales Press, forthcoming.

REVIEWS OF ARTICLES ON GILLIAN CLARKE

Ancestral Lines
1. Dale Jones, Don. *Books In Wales*. Aut. 93. p 13/4.
2. Mason, Neal. . *Bulletin of Welsh Academy 33*. March 1994.
3. Woods, Tim. 'Challenging the Establishment?' *Planet* 103, Feb./March 1994. pp102-3.

ARTICLES/ BOOKS INCLUDING COMMENT ON GILLIAN CLARKE

Aaron, Jane. 'Echoing the (M)other Tongue: *Cynghanedd* and the English Language Poet.' *'Fire Green As Grass': Studies of the Creative Impulse in Anglo-Welsh Poetry and Short Stories of the Twentieth Century.* Ed. Belinda Humfrey. Llandysul: Gomer, 1995. pp 1-23.

Anon. 'Carcanet'. *PNR* 13.6, 1987

Barker, Jonathan. 'Introduction'. *Poetry Book Society Anthology 1986/7.* Hutchinson, 1986.

Beddoe, Deirdre. 'Images of Welsh Women'.*Wales: The Imagined Nation.* Ed. Tony Curtis. p 227.

Brightmore, Gillian. '"Stonking" in the Valleys: An Exploration of Women Writing Poetry in Wales 1986-1996.' *Books In Wales*. Summer 1996 pp5-6.

Curtis, Tony. 'Grafting the Sour to Sweetness'. *Wales: The Imagined Nation.* Ed. Tony Curtis. Bridgend: Poetry Wales Press, 1987.
Curtis, Tony. (on 'The Hare') in *How to Study Modern Poetry.* Macmillan, 1990 pp 146-151.

Gifford, Terry. *Green Voices: understanding contemporary nature poetry.* Manchester: Manchester University Press, 1995.

Gifford, Terry. 'Have We Lost Our Nature Poets?' *Planet* 114. Dec./June 1995/6. pp 48-52.

Hughes, Ted. (a letter on multiple poets). *Times Literary Supplement* 1992, 4640, p 15.

Jenkins, Randal. 'The New Anglo-Welsh Poets'. *Poetry Wales* 8.2. 1972, pp 5-16.

Peach, Linden. "The Imagination's Caress': Identity and Symbolism in the Work of Gillian Clarke and Christine Evans.' *'Fire Green as Grass': Studies of the Creative Impulse in Anglo-Welsh Poetry and Short Stories of the Twentieth Century.* Ed. Belinda Humfrey. Llandysul: Gomer, 1995. pp 146-155.
Poole, Richard. 'Gender and Persona'. *Poetry Wales* 25.4. 1990.

Sansom, Peter. *Writing Poems.* (Bloodaxe Poetry handbooks:2) Newcastle upon Tyne: Bloodaxe Books, 1994.

Smith, Kenneth R. 'The Portrait Poem: Reproduction of Mothering'. *Poetry Wales* 24.1. 1988.
Smith, Kenneth R. 'Poetry of Place: The Haunted Interiors'. *Poetry Wales* 24.2.
Smith, Kenneth R. 'A Vision of the Future?'. *Poetry Wales* 24.3.
Smith, Kenneth R. 'Praise of the Past: the Myth of Eternal Return in Women Writers'. *Poetry Wales* 24.4. 1989.

Smith, Ken. 'Women, Criticism and the Anglo-Welsh'. *Poetry Wales* 20,3. 1985.

Thomas, M.Wynn. 'Prints of Wales: Contemporary Welsh Poetry in English'. *Poetry in the British Isles: Non-Metropolitan Perspectives.* Eds. Hans-Werner Ludwig and Lothar Fietz. Cardiff: University of Wales Press, 1995. pp 97-114.

REVIEWS OF ARTICLES/BOOKS INCLUDING COMMENT ON GILLIAN CLARKE

Fire Green As Grass.
Thomas, M.Wynn. *New Welsh Review 29*, 1995. pp 92-94.
Green Voices: understanding contemporary nature poetry.
1. Pugh, Sheenagh. *Poetry Wales.*31.2. 1995. pp 62-64.
2. Ross, Bruce Clunies. 'Greening Poetry.' *Planet* 114. Dec./ Jan. 1995/6. pp 103-105.

How Poets Work
Cunningham, James. *Books in Wales.* Winter 1996. pp 16-17.

Compiled by Diane Green

(with thanks to Professor M. Wynn Thomas and Gillian Clarke for their help).

Notes on Contributors

Dannie Abse is a novelist, poet and playwright with almost twenty titles to his name. Some of the most recent publications include *Selected Poems* (Penguin) and *On the Evening Road* (Hutchinson). He is editor of the forthcoming *Twentieth Century Anglo-Welsh Poetry* (Seren).

Elin ap Hywel
Poet, translator, editor of Honno (Welsh Women's Press) and Chairperson of Tŷ Newydd Writing Centre. The author of two volumes of poetry, *Cyfaddawdu* and *Pethau Brau*, she has recently contributed translations to Menna Elfyn's *Cell Angel* (1996) and *Eucalyptus* (1995).

Sally Baker worked as a language teacher in England and in Mexico before moving to North Wales. She has been the Director at Tŷ Newydd Writers' Centre, Llanystumdwy since it was established in 1990.

Tony Conran
His collections include *Blodeuwedd* (1988) and *Castles* (1993) as well as the more recent *All Hallows* (1995). His forth-coming publications include *Visions and Praying Mantids* and translation of the poetry of Waldo Williams, *The Peacemakers* (Gomer, 1997). In 1995 writers celebrated his work with a book called *Thirteen Ways of Looking at Tony Conran*.

Tony Curtis is a poet and professor of poetry at the University of Glamorgan. He is the author of numerous collections of poems, the most recent being *War Voices* (Seren, 1996) and a body of critical work which includes *The Art of Seamus Heaney* (1982) and *How Poets Work* (1996).

Menna Elfyn is author of seven collections of poetry which include *Eucalyptus* (Gomer) and *Cell Angel* (Bloodaxe). She has also written for stage and television. The two bilingual collections are the result of collaborations with several poet-translators, Gillian Clarke being one of them.

Christine Evans is author of four collections of poetry which include *Looking Inland* and *Island of Dark Horses*. She is the editor of two short story collections, *The Blue Man* and *Old Enough* (Pont Books), in which Gillian Clarke's stories appeared.

Diane Green is a Ph.D. student at University of Wales, Swansea, where she recently completed an M.A. in Modern Welsh Writing in English.

Seamus Heaney won the Nobel Prize winner for Literature in 1995. His most recent collection of poems is *The Spirit Level* (1996).

Greg Hill is Head of General Education at Coleg Ceredigion and was co-editor of the *Anglo-Welsh Review* with Gillian Clarke and subsequently editor. He has published poetry and criticism in various magazines.

Ted Hughes has been Poet Laureate since 1984. He has recently edited *The School Bag* (Faber & Faber), with Seamus Heaney.

Jeremy Hooker is poet and professor of English at Bath College and author of eight volumes. His most recent book of poems, *Their Silence a Language*, appeared in collaboration with the sculptor Lee Grandjean.

Hilary Llewelyn Williams is author of two volumes of poetry, *The Tree Calendar* (Poetry Wales Press) and *Book of Shadows* (Seren). Her new collection, *Animalculture*, is to be published by Seren in 1997.

Raymond Garlick has published nine books of poetry since 1950. Gomer published his *Collected Poems* in 1987 and *Travel Notes* in 1992. In 1995/6 a monograph on his work was published in the University of Wales Press's 'Writers of Wales' series.

Nigel Jenkins's books include *Acts of Union: Selected Poems 1975-89* (1990) and *Gwalia in Khasia* (1995), which won the Arts Council of Wales Book of the Year Prize for 1995. A cassette of his poems, *Remember Tomorrow*, was produced for an American tour of poetry in 1997.

Kathy Miles is one of the founding members of Lampeter Writers' Workshop. Her work has been published in numerous magazines and anthologies. She has published one volume of poetry, *The Rocking Stone* (Poetry Wales Press), and has edited an anthology, *The Third Day: Landscape and the Word* (Gomer).

Robert Minhinnick is author of six collections of poetry including *Hey Fatman* (1994). His first collection of essays, *Watching the Fire-Eaters*, won the Arts Council of Wales Book of the Year Prize in 1993. His second book of essays, *Badlands*, appeared in 1996.

M .Wynn Thomas is Professor of English at the University of Wales, Swansea. Among his numerous books are *Internal Difference: literature in twentieth century Wales* (1992) and *The Lunar Light of Whitman's Poetry*. More recent publications are *The Page's Drift: RS Thomas at eighty* and *Dail Glaswellt*, a Welsh translation of Walt Whitman's poetry.

R.S. Thomas is Wales's most distinguished writer with over 30 publications to his name. He was nominated for the Nobel prize for Literature in 1996.